RESTAURANT FOOD SERVICE EQUIPMENT

John A. Drysdale

Professor Emeritus

Johnson County Community College

Library of Congress Cataloging-in-Publication Data

Drysdale, John A.
    Restaurant food service equipment/John A. Drysdale.—1st ed.
      p. cm.
Includes index.
ISBN-13: 978-0-13-501788-3 (alk. paper)
ISBN-10: 0-13-501788-2 (alk. paper)
  1. Food service—Equipment and supplies. 2. Food service—Sanitation. I. Title.
TX912.D796 2010
642—dc22

2008051406

Editor in Chief: Vernon Anthony
Acquisitions Editor: William Lawrensen
Editorial Assistant: Lara Dimmick
Production Manager: Kathy Sleys
Full Service Project Management: Sadagoban Balaji/Integra Software Services
Art Director: Jayne Conte
Cover Designer: Margaret Kenselaar
Cover art/image/photo[s]: Getty Images, Inc.
Director of Marketing: David Gesell
Campaign Marketing Manager: Leigh Ann Sims
Curriculum Marketing Manager: Thomas Hayward
Marketing Assistant: Les Roberts

This book was set in Palatino by Integra and was printed and bound by Bind-Rite Graphics. The cover was printed by Demand Production Center.

Pearson Education Ltd., London
Pearson Education Singapore, Pte. Ltd.
Pearson Education Canada, Inc.
Pearson Education—Japan
Pearson Education Australia PTY, Limited

Pearson Education North Asia Ltd., Hong Kong
Pearson Educación de Mexico, S.A. de C.V.
Pearson Education Malaysia, Pte. Ltd.
Pearson Educacion Upper Saddle River,
   New Jersey

This publication presents information that has been gathered from manufacturers, government agencies, and others and is believed to be accurate and reliable. It is not intended to give legal, medical, or mechanical advice. Should such advice be required, the reader should seek competent legal, medical, or mechanical professionals for such advice. There is no guarantee of the accuracy of material presented, nor does the author or publisher assume any responsibility for damage or loss resulting from any errors or omissions.

Prentice Hall
is an imprint of

10 9 8 7 6 5 4 3 2 1
ISBN-13: 978-0-13-501788-3
ISBN-10:   0-13-501788-2

www.pearsonhighered.com

Dedicated to Jane, Judy, Jeanne, and Jackie

CONTENTS

PREFACE

Countless outbreaks of foodborne illness are traced to improper cleaning of equipment. Countless accidents in foodservice operations are caused by improper use of equipment. Countless dollars are wasted by repair and replacement of equipment that was not properly maintained.

This book is not intended as a primary course text but rather for use as a supplemental text. It is applicable for an introductory foods class, a sanitation and food safety course such as ServSafe, or in more advanced courses dealing with kitchen layout and design, equipment purchasing, or foodservice engineering. Conceivably, the student could therefore be expected to receive multiple uses out of a single book. The text explains how to properly clean, use, and maintain most of the major pieces of equipment in the kitchen. It is heavily illustrated to aid the student in comprehending the step-by-step procedures.

It begins with an introduction on the importance of the cleaning and sanitizing process, as well as covering basic cleaning materials, solutions, and supplies. The health department's role is also covered, giving specific examples of what they look for and why they look for it when inspecting an operation. Generalized health department regulations, standards, and inspection forms are given.

The function of safety is covered next. As most equipment is powered by either electricity or gas, their roles are examined. How the equipment works, terminology, why it is dangerous, how to avoid problems, how to light a pilot light and what to do when detecting gas leaks are also covered. In addition to electricity and gas, the section on safety also covers sharp objects such as knives and slicers, moving objects such as mixers and VCMs, and heat such as steam and deep fat fryers.

Maintenance is examined and the importance of properly maintaining equipment for longevity and to avoid costly repairs is also covered.

The next section covers specific pieces of equipment. It starts by giving an overview of that particular piece, explains in detail how to operate it, how to take it apart and put it back together, how to clean it, and the maintenance procedures to be used. The section is broken down by equipment type, including mechanical equipment, cooking equipment, refrigeration, and sanitation.

Each chapter begins with learning objectives and key terms. It concludes with questions, a project, a list of resources, bibliography, and key Web sites on equipment, sanitation, and safety that would be useful to the student. A competency verification sheet is also included at the end of the book.

This text is not only a useful addition to existing course texts in helping students understand the complexities of operating foodservice equipment but can also be used as an on-site reference text.

ACKNOWLEDGMENTS

A textbook is the work of many people, not just the author. The people listed below have given unselfishly of their time to review the manuscript and have provided the author with invaluable comments, suggestions, and criticisms. Their input has enhanced this work and is greatly appreciated: John Anton, University of Tennessee; Michael Carmel, Culinary Institute of Charleston; Jerald W. Chesser, California State Poly. University—Pomona; Nancy S. Graves, University of Houston; Dorothy Gunter, Bartlett, Illinois High School; Brian McDonald, Bellingham Technical College; Jeff Mekolites, Le Cordon Bleu of Culinary Arts Atlanta; Odette Smith-Ransome, Art Institute of Pittsburgh; Margaret E. Steiskal, Columbus State Community College; Gary S. Wilbers, Wilbers Manufacturers' Agents, Inc.; Jerry Vincent, Johnson County Community College, Emeritus; and Mike Zema, Elgin Community College.

ABOUT THE AUTHOR

John A. Drysdale is Professor Emeritus at Johnson County Community College, where he taught in the Hospitality Management department for 23 years. Prior to that, he was involved in multiunit restaurant management and has extensive experience in all facets of the foodservice industry, from fast food to fine dining. He has served as a consultant on many projects including kitchen design and layout, foodservice operations, and college curriculum development.

He is active in the Council of Hotel, Restaurant, and Institutional Education (CHRIE), having served as treasurer, regional chapter president, and on the board of directors representing associate degree programs. Drysdale has also been a member of the Commission of Accreditation for Hospitality Management Programs (CAHM) and has served as chair of the Commission.

Drysdale received a Bachelor of Arts Degree in Hotel and Restaurant Administration from Michigan State University and a Master of Science Degree in Administration from Central Michigan University. He is the author of *Profitable Menu Planning*, which is in its third edition, published by Prentice Hall.

CHAPTER 1

Cleaning, Sanitizing, and Maintaining Equipment

Objectives

Upon completion of this chapter, you will be able to:

- Understand the difference between cleaning and sanitizing.
- Know how often equipment needs to be cleaned and sanitized.
- Identify the three types of cleaning agents and tell the application of each.
- Explain the importance of the sanitation process.
- Differentiate between the three chemical sanitizing compounds.
- Explain the importance of equipment maintenance.
- Develop an equipment maintenance schedule.

Key Terms

abrasive cleaners
acid cleaners
chemical sanitizing
chlorine compounds
cleaning
degreasers
detergents

heat sanitization
iodine compounds
quaternary ammonium compounds
sanitizing
solvent cleaners
surfactants

INTRODUCTION

The cleaning and sanitizing of equipment is an important component in the overall food safety program in any kitchen operation. Potentially contaminated food comes into contact with equipment and utensils on a daily basis. Many times, different foods are processed on the same piece of equipment. Consider also that food is often processed at room temperature, which is well within the temperature danger zone. All these factors come together to form a potentially hazardous situation. To avoid an impending disaster from occurring, it is imperative that the equipment be properly cleaned and sanitized in a timely manner.

Notice that two words are being used: "cleaning" and "sanitizing." They are two separate and distinctly different processes that need to be properly completed to ensure a safe environment in which to prepare food. **Cleaning** is the process of removing visible soil. **Sanitizing** is the process of removing or reducing bacteria to a safe level. They are both necessary and one should not be done without the other.

How often equipment should be cleaned and sanitized depends on the equipment and what is being done with it. This subject will be covered with each specific piece of equipment in subsequent chapters. However, a general rule of thumb states that equipment should be cleaned and sanitized after each use. Additionally, it should be cleaned when a different type of food is being processed on the same piece of equipment. For example, if you were slicing meat on a slicer, it should be cleaned and sanitized prior to cutting vegetables. Under no circumstance should equipment, or parts of equipment, that comes into contact with food be allowed to sit for over four hours without being cleaned and sanitized. Equipment that is used but does not come in contact with food should be cleaned after each shift.

CLEANING

There are two steps to cleaning equipment: washing and rinsing. The washing process involves the use of a cleaning agent, of which there are three types: **detergent**s, **acid cleaners**, and **abrasive cleaners**.

Detergents

A detergent is a synthetic substance that comes in a liquid or dry (powder) form and is mixed with water. Always follow the manufacturer's directions regarding the amount of water to use when diluting the detergent. One of the major components of detergents is **surfactants**, which are agents designed to loosen the soil. The suds that we see when detergent and water are mixed are the vehicles that transport the surfactants.

There are several different types of detergents. Ones that are low in alkaline content are used on surfaces that contain new soil that has not hardened. These are often referred to as *mild detergents*. Worktables, floors, ceilings, and walls are normally cleaned with this type of detergent. Heavy-duty detergents are highly alkaline and are used where more stubborn soils need to be removed, such as burned-on food, heavy grease, or food dried on the surface. Dish washing machines use a heavy-duty detergent.

Another type of detergent is called a degreaser. This highly alkaline detergent also contains an agent that dissolves grease. **Degreasers**, unlike the two previously mentioned detergents, are not diluted with water and are normally used at full strength. They are used on griddles, ovens, and grills. Degreasers are sometimes classified as **solvent cleaners** as opposed to detergents.

Detergents can, particularly if not used in accordance with the manufacturer's directions, harm an employee's skin. Some people have an allergic reaction to detergents. Using rubber gloves when working with these agents is highly recommended.

Acid cleaners

These cleaners are used to loosen soils that detergents can't clean. They are also used on equipment where water is prevalent, such as steam tables, proofing cabinets, and dish machines. Most areas of the country have water that contain mineral deposits such as iron and/or lime which cause scaling. Acid cleaners are excellent in removing this scale. They are also used to remove rust stains as well as tarnish on silver, copper, or brass. These products should be handled carefully as they are designed to work on certain metals only and could damage other metals or surfaces. Before using an acid cleaner, make sure that its use is approved by the manufacturer for the surface material that you are working on. Since acid cleaners are quite potent, they could burn an employee's skin. Always use rubber gloves when cleaning with acid cleaners and always follow the manufacturer's instructions.

Abrasive cleaners

These use finely ground minerals such as silica to remove soil. Use abrasive cleaners with care as they can scratch the equipment surface, particularly if it is made of plastic or stainless steel. This is a heavy-duty cleaner and is used for food that has been encrusted or burned on. It is quite useful in the pot and pan area.

Cleaning agents do not remove the soil; they merely loosen it. Additional action, such as scrubbing or waterpower, is necessary to actually remove the soil. The longer the soil sets, the greater the action necessary to remove it. Wiping up spills immediately or washing a pot right after its use will result in a quicker and easier cleaning chore. Baked-on soil is also harder to clean. As scrubbing or water-power takes place, the outer layer of soil is removed, which allows the cleaning agent to attack the next layer of soil and loosen it. Another factor to consider in the cleaning process is the hardness of the water. Hard water reduces the cleaning agent's efficiency in loosening soil.

Remember that certain soils on some surfaces require certain cleaning agents. When choosing a cleaning agent, analyze the soil to be removed. Examine the surface. Is it plastic, stainless steel, wood? Choose the cleaning agent that is best suited for the soil and surface. Always read the manufacturer's directions. They will explain which materials the product can be used on and which ones it can't. Later in the text, the type of cleaning agent to use for each specific piece of equipment will be discussed.

Because they are caustic and poisonous if ingested, it is imperative that cleaning agents and chemical sanitizers be stored in their own storeroom or closet. They should be kept away from food storage areas. This will prevent any liquid or powder from coming into contact with food and contaminating it. Most health departments will require this.

After the cleaning of the equipment, it must be rinsed with clean water. This is very important. Detergent that is left on the surface could hinder the sanitation process, particularly if a chemical sanitizer is being used.

SANITIZING

After cleaning and rinsing, it is necessary to sanitize the equipment, utensils, or work surface. This is done to kill or reduce the number of bacteria to a safe level so that when food comes into contact with these objects, it will not become contaminated. Sanitizing can be accomplished by either applying heat or chemicals.

Heat sanitization

Heat sanitization is done with either steam or hot water. Specialized equipment is needed to conduct steam cleaning. Its cost and the fact that it is impractical on a daily basis limit its use to deep cleaning situations. For the most part when cleaning equipment, hot water sanitizing is also impractical; therefore, its use is normally limited to sanitizing utensils and dishes in dishwashers. To be effective, the water temperature should be a minimum of 180°F (83°C) with a total contact time of 30 seconds. Since most hot water systems are incapable of sustaining this temperature, a booster heater is employed on most hot temperature dish machines. (Note: Some dish machines, called low-temperature machines, employ chemical sanitizers rather than using heat as a sanitizing agent.)

When sanitizing equipment and work surfaces, as well as pot and pans, a chemical sanitizer is employed. The sanitizers most often used by foodservice operations can be broken down into three categories: **chlorine compounds**, **iodine compounds**, and **quaternary ammonium compounds**.

Chlorine compounds

A commonly used sanitizer, it works well in both hard and soft water. It is relatively inexpensive and does not leave a film on surfaces. A downside to using chlorine is that it can be harmful to some metals, causing corrosion to stainless steel and aluminum, particularly if it is not used in the proper concentration. The surface must be completely cleaned and thoroughly rinsed for chlorine to work properly as dirt and detergent tend to reduce its effectiveness. Water temperature should ideally be at 75°F (24°C) and certainly no higher than 115°F (46°C). Improper concentration can harm an employee's skin.

Iodine compounds

Iodine is not as effective as chlorine and is also more expensive. However, it works well in hard water. It is safe to use on all metal surfaces, but, if mixed improperly or used at a temperature over 120°F (49°C), iodine can cause corrosion. The concentration of iodine is indicated by color—the darker the color, the stronger the solution. Soil and detergent will not deter its effectiveness as much as chlorine. The temperature should be between 75°F (24°C) and 120°F (49°C). Properly mixed, it will not irritate an employee's skin.

Quaternary ammonium compounds

Commonly called quats, these compounds are safe to use on almost all equipment and metal surfaces. However, they do not work as well as the others do in hard water. While some detergents will reduce the effectiveness of certain quats, soil will not affect it as much as it affects chlorine. Ideal water temperature is 75°F (24°C). Properly mixed, it will not irritate an employee's skin.

The effectiveness of all sanitizing agents is affected by time and concentration. The amount of time that a sanitizing agent should be in contact with the surface being sanitized varies with the type of agent being used and the manufacturer of that agent. Check with your local health department and/or the manufacturer's recommendations to ascertain the correct amount of time that the sanitizing agent should be in contact with the equipment, utensil, or work surface. Additionally, the concentration should be measured with a test kit. These kits, which are available from your grocery supplier, are color-coded to indicate the strength of the solution. Do not exceed the recommended strength as damage to equipment or your skin could occur. In this case, more is not better.

EQUIPMENT MAINTENANCE

Equipment that is properly cleaned and sanitized will not only assure a safe environment for employees and customers, it will also lengthen the life of that equipment. In addition to keeping equipment clean and sanitary, it is also necessary to perform regular maintenance duties. One of the most overlooked aspects of foodservice management is the maintenance of equipment. In the day-to-day rush to get menus planned, food purchased, meals prepared, schedules made, and reports completed, maintenance is normally put off for a later day.

Since most maintenance is done on a periodic basis of every few months or yearly, it is often forgotten by the time the task is supposed to be completed. Part of the problem lies in the fact that foodservice equipment is so well built, it rarely breaks down. When it does, however, it does so at the worst possible time.

Instead of performing maintenance when it should be done, it gets done when it must be done. For example, if the glide on the slicer that moves the carriage does not get lubricated on a monthly basis, as the manufacturer recommends, it will eventually get done when it becomes increasingly difficult to move the carriage back and forth.

Sometimes, it is too late to perform the maintenance task. When the refrigerator stops working because the motor burned out . . . because the condenser fins were not vacuumed monthly . . . because nobody bothered to do it, it is too late. From a purely economic viewpoint, it takes less than 15 minutes to vacuum a condenser. Figuring $10 per hour labor to have someone do this, the cost is $2.50 each month. This is considerably less than the cost of a new motor plus installation, not to mention food spoilage, all of which could run into the thousands of dollars.

The solution to having a good maintenance program is to have a plan. By using a spreadsheet on your computer, this can become a simple task.

- In column one, list every piece of equipment in the operation.
- In column two, list the maintenance duty to be performed.
- In column three, list how often it needs to be performed.
- In column four, list the position or title of the person who is to perform that function.

By using the sort key on your computer, the spreadsheet can be separated by function. For example, the third column can be sorted and management can see readily how often each job needs to be done on each piece of equipment (see Figure 1.1).

Equipment	Maintenance to be performed	Timing
Steam-jacketed kettle	safety valve check	daily
Steam-jacketed kettle	jacket vacuum	daily
Steam-jacketed kettle	water level	daily
Dishwasher	check wash & rinse arms	daily
Refrigerator	check door gaskets	weekly
Range, gas	burner ports cleaned	weekly
Induction cooktops	filters cleaned	weekly
Proofing cabinet	water pan cleaned	weekly
Hot holding cabinet	water pan cleaned	weekly
Microwave oven	filters cleaned	weekly
Dishwasher, three tank	top cover & duct cleaned	bimonthly
Dishwasher, three tank	blower/dryer filter cleaned	bimonthly
Mixer, bowl lift	lubrication	monthly
Freezer	check door gaskets	monthly
Microwave oven	discharge vents cleaned	monthly
Impinger oven	clean oven interior	monthly
Impinger oven	clean air finger components	monthly
Walk-in coolers/freezers	check gaskets/heater wire	monthly
Walk-in coolers/freezers	check for missing plug buttons	monthly
Slicer	arm lubrication	quarterly
Refrigerator/freezer	clean condenser fins	monthly
Dishwasher	gas models check flue	quarterly
Carbonated beverage dispenser	check syrup lines for tags	quarterly
Carbonated beverage dispenser	check water:syrup ratio	quarterly
Carbonated beverage dispenser	clean condenser fins	quarterly
Carbonated beverage dispenser	service rep check system	quarterly
Impinger oven	vacuum blower motors	quarterly
Walk-in coolers/freezers	lubricate hinges	quarterly
Walk-in coolers/freezers	vacuum condenser coils	quarterly
Dishwasher, three tank	gear motor oil level	semiannually
Ice machine	cleaned and sanitized	semiannually
Ice machine	condenser cleaned	semiannually
Ice machine	checked for leaks	semiannually
Impinger oven	clean burner nozzles	semiannually
Impinger oven	clean venting system	semiannually
Impinger oven	check conveyer for wear	semiannually
Exhaust hood	clean hood and ductwork	semiannually
Fire suppressant system	checked	semiannually
Braising pan	trunnion bearings oiled	semiannually
Mixer, bowl clamps	lubrication	semiannually
Ovens	venting system	annually
Impinger oven	lubricate drive shaft bearings	annually
Braising pan	maintenance check	annually
Slicer	knife sharpening	as needed
Can opener	knife replacement	as needed
Food cutter	knives sharpened	as needed
Walk-in coolers/freezers	adjust defrost cycles	as needed
Oven steamer	de-lime	check manual

FIGURE 1.1

As you read through the text, you will see that the maintenance to be performed is listed with each piece of equipment. While maintenance is fairly standard between the different manufacturers and the different models of equipment, it is always wise to consult the owner's manual for the needed upkeep.

Because maintenance is out of the sphere of everyday operations, it is important to develop a discipline to assure that it is being carried out. Equipment costs for a small restaurant can run well over $100,000. With larger operations, such as hotel kitchens, this cost would run well over $1,000,000. This investment needs to be protected. It's like changing the oil in your car to protect the engine and your investment.

Questions

1. Explain the difference between cleaning and sanitizing. Is one more important than the other? Must one be done in conjunction with the other?
2. How often should equipment be cleaned? Why is it important to clean equipment on a timely basis?
3. Discuss the three types of cleaning agents and give an application for each.
4. Explain how chemical sanitizing and sanitizing with heat differ.
5. What are the three types of sanitizing compounds and what are their differences? Is one better than the other? Why?
6. Tell the importance of having and executing a maintenance schedule.

Group Project

Find a restaurant or foodservice operation in your neighborhood that does not have an equipment maintenance schedule and develop one for them.

Acknowledgments

Ecolab, St. Paul, MN.

Web Sites

Centers for Disease Control and Prevention
http://www.cdc.gov

Ecolab Inc.
http://www.ecolab.com

FDA Model Food Code
http://www.fda.gov

Occupational Safety and Health Administration (OSHA)
http://www.osha.gov

Resources

Longree, K. & Armbruster, G. (1996). Quantity Food Sanitation, 5th ed. New York, NY: John Wiley & Sons, Inc.

National Assessment Institute (1998). Handbook for Safe Food Service Management, 2nd ed. Upper Saddle River, NJ: Prentice Hall.

National Restaurant Association Education Foundation (1999). ServeSafe Coursebook. Chicago, IL: National Restaurant Association Education Foundation.

CHAPTER 2

Health Department's Role in Equipment Sanitation

Objectives

Upon completion of this chapter, you will be able to:

- Explain how the federal, state, and local governments interact to achieve a food safety inspection program.
- Discuss why, with a federal Model Food Code, there are so many differences and variances at the local level.
- Identify the various types of inspections that the health department conducts and the potential ramifications of each.
- Discuss the various methods the health department could use for grading and the various methods of reporting the grade to the community and the ramification of each.
- Demonstrate the importance of communication with the health inspector during and after the inspection.

Key Terms

citizen complaint inspection
Conference for Food Protection
disaster inspection
Food and Drug Administration (FDA)
HACCP

Model Food Code
new operation inspection
outbreak inspection
routine inspection

INTRODUCTION

One of the worst things that can happen to a restaurant or a foodservice operation is an outbreak of foodborne illness. To a restaurant depending on high sales and tight controls to make a profit, an outbreak could mean a loss of sales that would affect the bottom line and possible bankruptcy. If it is a nonprofit operation, such as a hospital or nursing home with high-risk clientele, the results could be devastating, causing complications to a patient's health or even death. At the very least, an outbreak will result in negative publicity, with the public loosing confidence in the operation. None of us wants this to happen to our business. While conscientious managers strive to run a safe operation along with all of their other duties of staffing, purchasing, training, menu development, production, service, and management, the task can be overwhelming. The good news is that the health department can help.

Quite often, the health department is viewed by management as the enemy. While a few egocentric inspectors would love to shut down a business to prove their stature, the vast majority of sanitarians are there to help you do a good job of guarding the public's safety. They are trained professionals whose knowledge should be utilized to run a safe and sanitary foodservice establishment. Look upon them as free consultants.

One of the health department's major roles in helping management run a safe operation includes using the proper cleaning techniques for equipment. This is very important since food can easily become contaminated from equipment that has not been properly cleaned. Misuse of equipment can also lead to cross-contamination. The health department's role does not stop with equipment; it goes far beyond that. Inspectors check temperatures; cleanliness of walls, floors, and ceilings; infestation control; HACCP-based inspections; sanitation training; and a myriad of other particulars. Because discussion here is limited to equipment, do not preclude that their responsibility is limited to this one area.

FEDERAL INVOLVEMENT

The local food inspector, or sanitarian, is the last link in a chain that makes up the food service inspection system. It all starts at the federal level with the **Food and Drug Administration (FDA),** which is responsible for the Model Food Code. The Code is based on contributions from the **Conference for Food Protection.** This conference is made up of foodservice professionals, sanitarians, scientists, researchers, and others who are involved with the discipline of food safety. Once their input is received, the FDA then goes about the task of rewriting and updating the Code every two years. Figure 2.1 is a model food establishment inspection report that is recommended by the FDA and is used by many local health departments. It is but one example of the conference results. Areas covered in the Model Food Code that are of interest to the foodservice industry include:

- Management and personnel—Covers the supervisor's role in the knowledge of food safety, employee's health, and personal cleanliness including hands, arms, fingernails, jewelry, and clothing, as well as hygienic practices.
- Food—Covers the condition of food in the establishment, sources, receiving procedures, protection from contamination after receiving, temperature control, destruction of organisms, limitation of organism growth, food presentation and menu representation, disposition of contaminated food, and special requirements for highly susceptible populations.
- Equipment and utensils—Covers equipment and utensil design and construction, equipment capacity, location, installation, maintenance, operation, cleaning procedures, and sanitation procedures.
- Linens—Covers the laundering and storage of linens
- Water, plumbing, and waste—Covers water source and quality, plumbing system, mobile food establishment water, sewage, and refuse facilities.
- Physical facilities—Covers materials for construction and repair, design, hand washing facilities, toilets, and maintenance.
- Poisonous or toxic materials—Covers proper labeling and container quality, storage, medicine, and first aid supplies.
- Compliance and enforcement—Covers code requirements and variances, plan submission and approval for new operations, construction inspection and approval, permits to operate, inspection frequency, correction of violations including imminent health hazard, critical and non-critical violations, and prevention of foodborne disease transmission by employees.

An important part of the Code is the Hazard Analysis Critical Control Point (HACCP) system. It is a system that monitors all of the sections of the Food Code in

DEPARTMENT OF HEALTH AND HUMAN SERVICES
PUBLIC HEALTH SERVICE
FOOD AND DRUG ADMINISTRATION

FOOD ESTABLISHMENT INSPECTION REPORT

Violations cited in this report shall be corrected within the time frames specified below, but within a period not to exceed 10 calendar days for critical items (§ 8-405.11) or 90 days for noncritical items (§ 8-406.11).

VIOLATIONS: **CRITICAL** _____   **NONCRITICAL** _____

ESTABLISHMENT:		**PERMIT NUMBER:**	**DATE:**
ADDRESS:	**CITY:**	**STATE:** **ZIP:**	
PERSON IN CHARGE / TITLE:		**TELEPHONE:**	
INSPECTOR / TITLE:			
INSPECTION TYPE: ROUTINE FOLLOW-UP COMPLAINT OTHER:		**TIME:**	

Critical (X)	Repeat (X)	Code Reference	Violation Description / Remarks / Corrections

Food Establishment Inspection Report Page ___ of ___

FIGURE 2.1   The FDA model food establishment inspection report.

Courtesy of the Department of Health and Human Services, Public Health Service, Food and Drug Administration.

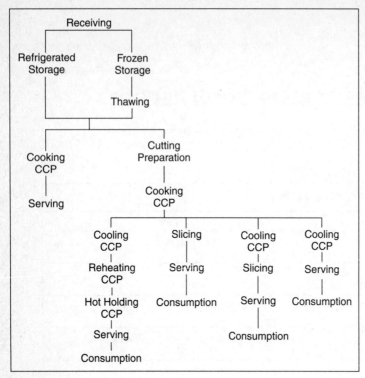

FIGURE 2.2   A model of a HACCP flow chart showing critical control points (CCP) from the receiving function to consumption.

Source: Federal Food & Drug Administration.

a particular foodservice establishment and combines it with a recordkeeping process to ensure that safe food is being served. There are seven principles of an effective **HACCP** plan:

1. Identify potential hazards.
2. Establish critical control points (CCP).
3. Define critical control (CCP) limits.
4. Monitor procedures.
5. Take corrective action.
6. Plan verification and modification.
7. Create documentation.

While the establishment of a HACCP plan is beyond the scope of this text, it is mentioned here because clean and sanitary equipment that is properly maintained is a significant part of the plan. Figure 2.2 shows a model HACCP flow chart that traces a product from the receiving function all the way through to service.

The Model Food Code is only a guide. It is not a law that each and every foodservice establishment must follow. Its purpose is to guide states and other local governmental agencies in enacting their own laws in regard to food safety.

STATE INVOLVEMENT

All states have laws regarding the health and safety of their citizens; however, not all states have the same law. Here is where all of the "exceptions to the rule" start. Since the Model Food Code is merely a guide, each state tends to treat it differently.

Some states have adopted the Model Food Code in its entirety and enacted it into law intact. Other states have modified the Code, taking into account particular circumstances that would affect it locally and enacting a modified version into law. Still other states have ignored the Code completely and written their own standards. Thus, while the majority of states embrace the majority of the Code, not all of them have embraced the Code in its entirety.

In some areas, cities and/or counties have developed their own codes. For the most part, these also follow, more or less, the Model Food Code. Often, the local law is stronger than the state law.

LOCAL INVOLVEMENT

While most states have a health department and a state law, the vast majority of them delegate the *enforcement* of the law to local jurisdictions. A local jurisdiction could be a city, township, county, or parish. In rural areas where there is no local authority or there are too few foodservice operations to warrant the expense of having a local health department, the state normally takes over the enforcement of the law.

In some areas, both the state and the local jurisdiction will inspect an operation. This can be confusing to the operator because the state inspector is following the state code and the local inspector is following the local code. Even if the codes are identical, the subjectivity of interpretation comes into play. The person who manages such an operation can experience much stress and frustration (see Figure 2.3).

HEALTH DEPARTMENT
KANSAS CITY, MISSOURI
FOOD PROTECTION PROGRAM

FOOD ESTABLISHMENT INSPECTION REPORT

FROZEN DESERT MACHINE	SMOKING ORD. COMLIANCE
☐ YES ☐ NO	☐ YES ☐ NO

BASED ON AN INSPECTION THIS DAY, THE ITEMS NOTED BELOW IDENTIFY NONCOMPLIANCE IN OPERATIONS OR FACILITIES WHICH MUST BE CORRECTED BY THE NEXT ROUTINE INSPECTION, OR SUCH SHORTER PERIOD OF TIME AS MAY BE SPECIFIED IN WRITING BY THE REGULATORY AUTHORITY. FAILURE TO COMPLY WITH ANY TIME LIMITS FOR CORRECTIONS SPECIFIED IN THIS NOTICE MAY RESULT IN CESSATION OF YOUR FOOD OPERATIONS. A FEE WILL BE ASSESSED FOR EACH RE INSPECTION.

P.H. PRIORITY   H   M   L

ESTABLISHMENT NAME	PERSON IN CHARGE	OWNERS NAME	PHONE
ADDRESS	DISTRICT	COUNTY	FAX
CITY/ZIP	ESTAB. NO.		

PURPOSE
☐ FIELD VISIT ☐ ROUTINE
☐ PRE-OPENING ☐ COMPLAINT
☐ REINSPECTION
☐ INVESTIGATION
☐ OTHER _____

WATER SUPPLY
☐ COMMUNITY
☐ NONCOMMUNITY Results_____
☐ PRIVATE   Date Sampled_____

SEWAGE DISPOSAL
☐ PUBLIC   ☐ PRIVATE

ESTABLISHMENT TYPE

☐ RESTAURANT ☐ RETAIL GROCERY/MARKET ☐ TRUCK SALES (PHF) ☐ ICE CREAM VENDOR
☐ MOBILE/PUSHCART ☐ USDA SUMMER FP INSTITUTION ☐ TAVERN ☐ BAKERY
☐ TEMP. FOOD STAND ☐ SCHOOL (PUBLIC) ☐ SCHOOL (PRIVATE)

FOOD PRODUCT	TEMP.	STORAGE LOCATION	FOOD PRODUCT	TEMP.	STORAGE LOCATION

FOOD CODE REFERENCES

2 MANAGEMENT/PERSONNEL
2-1 Supervision
2-2 Employee Health
2-3 Personal Cleanliness
2-4 Hygienic Practices

3 FOOD
3-1 Characteristics
3-2 Sources, Containers & Records
3-3 Protection from Contamination
3-4 Cooking & Reheating
3-5 Limiting Growth of Organisms
3-6 Food Presentation & Labeling
3-7 Contaminated Food

4 EQUIP., UTENSILS & LINENS
4-1 Materials for Construction
4-2 Design & Construction
4-3 Numbers & Capacities
4-4 Location & Installation
4-5 Maintenance & Operation
4-6 Cleaning
4-7 Sanitation
4-8 Laundering
4-9 Protection of Clean Items

5 WATER, PLUMBING & WASTE
5-1 Water
5-2 Plumbing
5-3 Mobile Water Tanks
5-4 Sewage & Liquid Waste
5-5 Refuse & Recycle/Returnables

6 PHYSICAL FACILITIES
6-1 Materials for Construction
6-2 Design & Construction
6-3 Numbers & Capacities
6-4 Location & Placement
6-5 Maintenance & Operation

7 POISONOUS OR TOXIC ITEMS
7-1 Labeling & Identification
7-2 Supplies & Applications
7-3 Storage & Display

CRITICAL ITEMS

Code Reference	Description: These items relate directly to factors which lead to foodborne illness. These items MUST RECEIVE IMMEDIATE ACTION within 72 hours or as stated.	Correct by (date)	Initial

NON-CRITICAL ITEMS

Code Reference	Description: These items relate to maintenance of food operations and cleanliness. These are to be corrected by the next regular inspection or as stated.	Correct by (date)	Initial

COMMENTS:

RECEIVED BY ▶	NAME AND TITLE			DATE
INSPECTED BY ▶	NAME	SAN. I.D. #	PHONE/FAX	TIME IN / TIME OUT

FIGURE 2.3 A Food Establishment Inspection Report based on the FDA Model.

Courtesy of the Kansas City Missouri Health Department.

WHEN THE HEALTH DEPARTMENT INSPECTS

Why and when the health department decides to inspect your operation at a particular time depends on many factors. First and foremost is the budget under which the local health department has to operate. The budget often reflects the values of the community. If health and safety are a local priority, the department usually has an adequate budget. If not, it operates with a tight budget, resulting in fewer inspections and overall less compliance from the foodservice industry (see Figure 2.4).

There are several different types of inspections. The type of inspection will determine how often the establishment will be inspected and more particularly what it is the inspector is looking for.

Routine inspection

This is a periodic inspection designed to make sure that the restaurant or foodservice operation is adhering to the standards set forth by the state law. It normally consists of the inspector looking over the entire operation, including receiving, storage, production, ware washing, and service. "Periodic" can mean monthly, quarterly, semiannually, or annually—or something else. Some jurisdictions require a definite number of visits per year, some recommend a number, and some leave it up to the inspector. Regardless of how often an operation is inspected, it is almost always unannounced.

The type of business being conducted by the foodservice operation can also be brought into play. Hospitals and nursing homes with a highly susceptible clientele could be inspected more often than fast-food restaurants with disposable wares. Serious violations during an inspection of any operation will trigger a re-inspection, sometimes within hours of the original inspection.

Citizen complaint

This brings a swift response from the health department. Complaints can cover anything from a customer seeing evidence of pest infestation, unhygienic practices by an employee, hair in the food, unsafe food temperatures, dirty operations, or one of many others. Inspectors will first verify that the complaint is justified and, if so, set up a corrective action program. Normally, there is a follow-up to see if the corrective actions are being followed. They may also conduct a routine inspection while they are there. Rest assured that if the complaint is justified, your routine inspections will automatically become more frequent.

Outbreak

This also brings a swift response. An outbreak of foodborne illness is a serious matter. The health inspector wants to know exactly what food caused the outbreak and have it analyzed to determine the exact type of illness. They also want to know what caused the food to become contaminated in the first place. Normally a HACCP inspection is conducted to determine this. Once determined, controls are set in place to assure that another outbreak will not occur. Unfortunately, this is too little, too late, since the damage has already been done to your customers and to your business.

Disaster

Should an ill-fated disaster, such as a fire, flood, or ice storm, strike your foodservice operation, the health department will be there shortly. (In one such instance, familiar to the author, where a local restaurant caught on fire, the health department actually arrived before the fire department.)

Their role is to ascertain that all food that was damaged is disposed of properly. Often there is a lack of electricity and therefore no refrigeration, with

OP

Search the OPCITY Site

GOVERNING BODY | CITY MANAGER | CALENDAR | HUMAN RESOURCES| NEWS | PARKS & REC. | POLICE | PUBLIC WORKS
PLANNING & DEVELOPMENT | HEALTH & ENVIRONMENT | CITY ATTORNEY | CITY CLERK | FINANCE | MUNICIPAL COURT

Food Establishment Inspection Report
Overland Park, KS 66210

Inspection Type: Routine
Inspection Date: Wednesday, October 10, 2001
Re-Inspection Scheduled For: Tuesday, October 16, 2001

Temperature Observations		
Food Product	**Temperature**	**Storage Location**
butter	75	table tops
white sauce	142	steam unit
tomato	55	right cook prep top

Critical Violations			
have a higher potential to contribute to foodborne illness			
Violation	**Title**	**Correct By**	**Remarks**
4-703.11	Hot Water and Chemical.*	10/16/2001	dishmachine out of sanitizer - do not use until properly primed
7-201.11	Separation.*	10/10/2001	chemical (Windex) stored on servers' prep area (Corrected during inspection)
3-202.11	Temperature.*	10/16/2001	butter (dairy product) may not be left out on the tables at room temperature - must be kept under 41 degrees or use an all oil margarine spread cooks unit running too warm on top - ice water must surround food pans at level of food REPEAT

Non-Critical Violations			
less likely than critical violations to directly contribute to foodborne illness			
Violation	**Title**	**Correct By**	**Remarks**
3-303.11	Ice Used as Exterior Coolant, Prohibited as Ingredient.	10/16/2001	do not store drinks in ice used for beverages at bar. 3rd REPEAT, (but not a critical so you get 1 more chance before penalized)
3-305.11	Food Storage.	10/10/2002	food on floor in walk-in freezer under shelving - must be 6" up (Corrected during inspection)
3-302.12	Food Storage Containers, Identified with Common Name of Food.	1/8/2002	label back colored food storage containers

FIGURE 2.4 An example of a health department's Web site which is used to communicate to the general public how a particular foodservice establishment adheres to established sanitation practices. Note the number of repeat violations on this report.

Courtesy of the Overland Park Kansas Health Department.

4-903.11	Equipment, Utensils, Linens, and Single-Service and Single-Use Articles.	1/8/2002	cutting boards may not be stored on the floor - rewash/sanitize and store 6" up knives may not be stored in the cracks between equipment (kitchen B) rewash/sanitize and store properly
6-402.11	Convenience and Accessibility.	1/8/2002	bar handsink blocked from use with misc items
6-202.15	Outer Openings, Protected.	1/8/2002	both back doors to the outside need the bottom gap sealed to prevent rodent/insect entry
6-303.11	Intensity.	1/8/2002	all florescent fixtures over food prep areas need all 4 bulbs installed at the highest wattage the fixture can handle to maintain the new code requirement of 50 foot candles of intensity replace any burned out bulbs in the hood

Comments:

Watch your REPEAT violations as if they are critical or marked several inspections, it could result in a Notice to Appear in Court. These would include your cooks refrigeration unit temperatures/drinks kept at bar in ice used for beverages/door self-closer for employee restroom/boxed single service items stored on the floor/soap and paper towels/butters out at room temperature on the tables/raw meats improperly stored/lighting issues.......Any of these marked on the next inspection could result in a fine for each violation noted. This is your final warning to resolve these issues well or you will receive a Notice to Appear in Court**********

The full Kansas Food Code can be viewed here. (.pdf format, 532K)

City Home	Food Service	Establishment Search

The Health & Environment Division may be contacted by phone at 913/895-6270 or by e-mail at health@opkansas.org

Questions? Comments? E-mail city@opkansas.org

FIGURE 2.4 (Continued)

potentially dangerous foods being within the temperature danger zone guidelines. In addition to overseeing the disposal of the potentially infected food, they will also assess the physical damage to the kitchen and storage areas and advise you as to what needs to be done to reopen.

New operation

Prior to the building of the foodservice operation, the health department will review the plans. They must sign off on the plans prior to a building permit being issued. When the building is ready for occupancy, they will conduct an inspection. In most jurisdictions, this inspection must take place prior to any food being delivered, and it is also necessary to pass this inspection before an occupancy license is issued. Normally this is a lengthy and detailed inspection, because the health department wants the operator to get started on the right track. In some instances, the sanitarian will conduct a seminar for all your employees on safe food handling practices.

WRITTEN REPORT

After the inspection, the inspector normally goes over the results of the assessment with the unit manager. In all cases, there is a written report. One copy stays with the foodservice operation, a copy is filed at the health department, and the inspector keeps a copy. The style and makeup of the report vary by jurisdiction. Some use a written report in which the violation is explained and is tied into a code standard. Others use a checklist in which the standards are listed on the report and the violations are simply checked. It is important to remember that a violation is always tied to a standard of the code.

In some areas the written reports are graded. Some use a letter grade, some a number grade, and some no grade at all, merely citing the violations. Some require the grade (if given) to be posted in a conspicuous public place in the establishment. Some post the grades in the local newspaper or on the Web. Regardless of how the report is designed, the grade is weighted. That is, some items receive a higher weight or value depending on the nature of the violation. For example, food sitting in the steam table at 100°F (38°C) is a more serious violation than a pile of dust swept into the corner. That is not to say that any violation is not serious, just that some violations pose a greater danger to food safety and therefore have a greater need to be corrected immediately.

When inspectors go over the report, they will discuss the violations with the manager. During this discussion, they should give suggestions to correct the violation. Simple corrections should be taken care of immediately during the inspector's visit. For example, an employee can be directed to fill the empty soap dispenser at the hand sink. Later, a control mechanism delegating responsibility can be set in place to prevent the dispenser from becoming empty.

The inspector will also give a time frame for correcting some of the more serious violations. Several will need to be corrected by the next visit; others will need to be corrected now. A re-inspection could be set up for the next day or even in a few hours. For example, the food in the steam table at 100°F (38°C) should be discarded and replaced with a properly prepared, properly heated product. The question now becomes what happened to cause the food to be held within the danger zone? At what temperature is the steam table set? Is it working properly? Who is responsible? What is the control mechanism? These questions should be addressed immediately because the serving temperature is a critical issue. The health department will re-inspect soon. Count on it.

Questions

1. Trace the chain of events that take place from the federal government to the state government to the local government that evolve into the health inspection in your restaurant.
2. What are the main components of the Model Food Code?
3. Differentiate between the different types of health department inspections that could be done in your foodservice operation. Tell why each is important. Does one carry more weight than the other?
4. Discuss the ramifications of making the public aware of a restaurant's inspection grade. Frame your discussion from both the public's perspective and the operator's perspective.
5. What is HACCP and why is it important?

Project

Obtain a blank inspection sheet from your local health department or copy the inspection sheet in this chapter.

Conduct a mock inspection of your food lab at school or at your place of employment.

Acknowledgments

The Food and Drug Administration, Washington, DC.
Health Department, Kansas City, MO.
Health Department, Overland Park, KS.

Web Sites

FDA Model Food Code
http://www.fda.gov

Occupational Safety and Health Administration (OSHA)
http://www.osha.gov

Overland Park KS Health Department
http://www.opkansas.org

Resources

Food & Drug Administration (2001). Model Food Code. Washington, DC: United States Government, Food and Drug Administration.

Longree, K. & Armbruster, G. (1996). Quantity Food Sanitation, 5th ed. New York, NY: John Wiley & Sons, Inc.

National Assessment Institute (1998). Handbook for Safe Food Service Management, 2nd ed. Upper Saddle River, NJ: Prentice Hall.

National Restaurant Association Education Foundation (1999). ServeSafe Coursebook. Chicago, IL: National Restaurant Association Education Foundation.

Schumann, M., Schneid, T., Schumann, B., & Fagel, M. (1997). Food Safety Law. New York, NY: Van Nostrand Reinhold.

CHAPTER 3

Safe Equipment Operation

Objectives

Upon completion of this chapter, you will be able to:

- Discuss safety issues regarding cuts from knives, blades, and broken glass.
- Demonstrate the proper procedure for handling a gas leak.
- Explain the steps necessary to prevent carbon monoxide from becoming a problem in the foodservice operation.
- Identify a circuit breaker box and explain the importance of disconnecting the source of electricity prior to cleaning or repairing a piece of electrical equipment.
- Demonstrate the correct fire extinguisher to use depending on the type of fire as well as the correct technique for extinguishing the fire.
- Know what actions to take in the event of an accident in the foodservice establishment.

Key Terms

carbon monoxide
circuit box tag
circuit breaker
Class A, B, C, and K fires
Hazard Communication Standard (HCS)

Heimlich maneuver
Material Safety Data Sheets (MSDS)
mercaptan
Occupational Safety and Health
Administration (OSHA)

INTRODUCTION

The kitchen is a dangerous place. As a manager, you have a large responsibility to make sure that workplace is as safe as it can be for employees and customers. This applies not only to the equipment being properly installed and maintained, but also to personal behavior. Employees need to be trained in the correct use of the equipment and also taught to work in a professional manner with no horseplay. Most accidents are the result of management's inattention to detail or employee error.

SHARP OBJECTS

While knives are most often the culprit regarding cuts, other sources can also contribute to this type of mishap. Blades on slicers, cutter mixers, and choppers can cause cuts that are often more severe than knife cuts.

Proper knife-handling procedures are important in managing a safe kitchen.

- Keep the knife sharp. It is common knowledge that a dull blade makes it harder to cut a product. With a dull knife, the user exerts more pressure on the knife, resulting in the knife or product slipping and cutting the user.
- Always cut on a flat, stable surface. If using a cutting board, place a damp cloth under the board to stabilize it. Cut uneven or round objects in half, so that they have a flat surface.
- Cut away from the body rather than toward it, especially when carving a roast or performing a boning procedure.
- If a knife falls, jump away from it. Our natural reaction is to grab objects that fall. Train yourself not to do this with knives.
- Wash the knives immediately after use. Never, never, never, never, never leave a knife in a sink to soak. The person who comes after you to wash utensils will never forgive you.
- Always store knives in a knife rack. Do not store them loose in drawers with other utensils.

An additional source of cuts is broken glass. Always use a brush or broom along with a dustpan to clean up broken glass. Never use your hands. If glass breaks over or around food, immediately throw the entire product away. Many kitchens follow the policy of having employees in the production area use plastic cups rather than glasses for their beverages. If a glass breaks in an ice bin (it shouldn't because you should have used the ice scoop), remove all of the ice and clean the bin with warm water.

GAS

Ranges, ovens, fryers, griddles, steam kettles, and other cooking appliances are all potential sources for accidents. This equipment, for the most part, is powered by gas, electricity, or steam, while some grills use wood or charcoal for their heat source. While the vast majority of accidents from this equipment are burns, other mishaps can also happen.

Gas leaks, for example, can cause an explosion. While this is a very rare occurrence, when it does happen, it is often violent and deadly. The best way to detect escaping gas is by smell. Gas in its natural state has no odor; however, the utilities that distribute natural gas have added **mercaptan**, an odorant that smells like sulfur or rotten eggs. If you detect this smell:

- Clear the building of all employees and customers.
- Call 911 or your local fire and/or police department on a neighboring business's phone or on your cell phone away from the building. Do not use the phone in the building because you could set off an explosion.
- Do not turn any electrical switches or any equipment on or off.
- Do not return to the building until authorized to do so by the authorities.

Posters that are available from your local gas service company will be useful in explaining to your employees exactly what to do should such an occurrence take place.

Another rare but deadly hazard is **carbon monoxide**. This occurs when natural gas, propane gas, wood, or charcoal is improperly or incompletely burned. Unlike raw natural gas, carbon monoxide is odorless. Symptoms of exposure to carbon monoxide are flu-like symptoms, including headaches, drowsiness, and/or a nauseous feeling. Other symptoms include ringing in the ears, blurred vision, or chest pains. The longer the exposure to carbon monoxide, the worse the symptoms become, and it could lead to brain damage and death. To prevent creating carbon monoxide:

- Ascertain that the gas equipment in your operation has been installed correctly.
- Have gas equipment inspected annually for proper operation.

- Ascertain that wood or charcoal grills and all gas equipment are properly ventilated.
- Have flues from hot water heaters and furnaces checked annually for obstructions.

Carbon monoxide detectors have been used with mixed results in commercial foodservice operations. Should you purchase these, make sure that they are approved by the American Gas Association and the Gas Research Institute.

ELECTRICAL

In addition to hazards from gas equipment, there are hazards from all electrical equipment in general, not just cooking appliances. To avoid electrocution:

- Ascertain that all electrical equipment is properly installed. Check local codes to see if 200-volt and 400-volt equipment needs to be directly wired.
- Make sure that all electrical equipment is properly grounded.
- Check for frayed wires.
- Water and electricity do not mix. When cleaning electrical equipment use a damp (not wet) cloth. Do not immerse motors or pumps in water.
- Make sure that all circuit breaker boxes are correctly labeled and that your employees know the location(s) of these boxes. **Circuit breakers** do exactly what their name implies: They break the circuit of electricity from the line coming into the kitchen and going on to each piece of equipment. Should a line become overloaded, they automatically shut off (break) the circuit. They can be manually shut off by flipping the switch to the OFF position, thus stopping the flow of electricity to the equipment (or pieces of equipment) serviced by that particular breaker.
- Do not attempt to clean or work on any piece of electrical equipment without first disconnecting the plug. If the equipment is direct-wired, shut off the circuit breaker at the electrical panel box.
- When shutting off power at the circuit box, use a circuit breaker tag to alert others that someone is working on the equipment. Often, more than one piece of equipment is on a circuit. A serious injury could result if someone working with another piece of equipment on the same circuit flips the switch back on.

BURNS

The vast majority of accidents in commercial kitchens come from burns. Using common sense and paying attention to detail can avoid most burns.

- Open oven and steamer doors slowly to allow heat and vapors to escape.
- Lift pot lids slowly using the handle. Tilt the lid up and away so that the surface of the lid protects you from the steam.
- Get help when removing heavy stockpots from the range. Confirm that both of you are aware of where you are going before you start. Also make sure that the floor is not slippery and is free of objects that can be tripped on.
- Make sure that pot holders are heavy duty and dry. Do not use cleaning cloths for this purpose.
- Saucepan handles should not hang over the edge of the range.
- Make sure that steam escape pipes are located away from traffic isles.

For the most part, avoiding burns is not rocket science, just common sense.

FIRE SAFETY

The very nature of the foodservice business is that fire is a daily possibility. Hot oil in deep fat fryers, open flame on gas ranges, open fire on broilers and grills, high voltage electrical equipment, and cigarettes in the dining room and the employees break room all meet the criteria to cause a fire. When a fire does break out, two things need to happen immediately and simultaneously, and both of them are critical.

First, call the fire department (911) without delay even if the fire is small and you intend to put it out yourself. Minutes are critical with a fire. If you are successful in putting out the fire and the firefighters arrive—fine. On the flip side, if you are not successful and then call, precious minutes have been lost and the damage is great.

Second, everyone—employees and customers—should be removed from the building. This should be done in a calm and orderly manner. Since all of this is happening at once, you cannot do it yourself. You need a plan. Responsibilities should be delegated by position—not by person. People change (especially with multiple shifts) but positions for the most part do not. A drawing should be made of the establishment showing all exits, routes to use to access those exits, and an alternate route in case an exit is blocked. The drawing should be posted throughout the building. The plan should be practiced by all employees on a regularly recurring basis. New employees should be made aware of the plan, including their area of responsibility. Figure 3.1 shows an example of a fire evacuation plan.

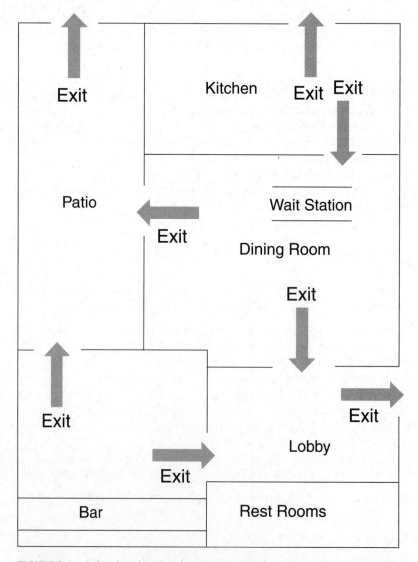

FIGURE 3.1   A drawing showing the escape routes for customer and employees in a restaurant. Every foodservice operation should have one and practice it periodically.

FIGURE 3.2 Icons used to specify the class of fire on the fire extinguisher. Make sure you use the correct extinguisher for the type of fire to be suppressed.

Source: Occupational Safety and Health Administration.

CLASS A, B, C, AND K FIRES

In foodservice operations there are four primary classifications of fire:

- A **Class A fire** is one that occurs with ordinary materials such as wood, paper, or cloth (see Figure 3.2).
- A **Class B fire** occurs with flammable liquids (see Figure 3.2).
- A **Class C fire** is an electrical fire (see Figure 3.2).
- A **Class K fire** is a fire that involves vegetable oils, animal oils, or fats (see Figure 3.2).

It should be noted that Class B fires used to include grease fires; however, in 1998, grease fires were removed from Class B and given their own classification of Class K. It is important to know the different fire classes because different chemicals are used to extinguish different classes. For example, while one fire extinguisher will put out an electrical fire, it should not be used on a grease fire. Fire extinguishers are clearly marked as to which types of fire they will extinguish. Some are made to put out more than one class of fire. Not only is it important to know which one to use, it is also necessary to know where to place the extinguishers.

- Class A extinguishers should be placed throughout the foodservice operation.
- Class B extinguishers should be placed by the cook's line and where flammable liquids such as cleaning agents are stored.
- Class C extinguishers should be located near electrical motors and transformers.
- Class K extinguishers should be located near deep fat fryers, tilt skillets, and sauté areas.

Their exact locations, as well as how many and how far apart they should be, is mandated by law in most jurisdictions. The general rule is that travel distance to a fire extinguisher should not be more than 75 feet. The extinguisher should be visible from a distance of 50 feet. Since specific laws vary, consult with your local fire department on the proper placement of extinguishers in your operation.

It is important to train all your employees in the proper procedure to employ when using an extinguisher. You never know when and where a fire will break out and who will be the most logical person to put it out. A picture of an extinguisher is given in Figure 3.3. Using the word **PASS** will help you remember the correct procedure to use the extinguisher:

P—Pull the pin. Hold the extinguisher with the nozzle pointing away from you and release the locking mechanism.

A—Aim low. Point the extinguisher at the base of the fire.

S—Squeeze the lever slowly and evenly.

S—Sweep the nozzle from side to side.

FIGURE 3.3 A diagram showing the parts of a portable fire extinguisher.

Source: Occupational Safety and Health Administration (OSHA).

Local fire departments will give demonstrations on the correct process. Make sure that all extinguishers are properly marked with a sign above them on the wall to designate their location. Fire extinguishers should be checked periodically, normally once a year, by a reputable company. The date of the inspection should be noted on a tag attached to the extinguisher. State and local law normally specify how often inspections should occur.

FIRST AID

There will be accidents in any foodservice operation. Dangerous equipment, excessive heat and steam, open flame, sharp edges, and the possibility of choking all spell misfortune from time to time. The astute manager is ready for them when they do happen by knowing what to do. Management and key employees should all be trained in first aid. Courses are available from the Red Cross, local hospitals, EMT services, and community colleges. Lists of emergency phone numbers should be posted on all phones and include:

- 911.
- Fire, police, and ambulance (if different from 911).
- Health department.
- Hospital.
- Poison control center.
- Manager's home phone number.

While many foodservice injuries are minor in nature and can be handled in-house, if it is a marginal situation, make the call. Defining "marginal" is hard to do. A simple knife cut, while appearing minor, could be deeper than it seems or the person's blood may not coagulate readily. If you have any doubt, notify 911. It is better to err on the side of caution.

Several first aid kits should be located throughout the kitchen and dining areas. They should be properly stocked to take care of minor cuts and burns. Monthly, or more often if necessary, replenish any products that have been removed from the kit. The American Red Cross recommends that at a minimum you should have the following supplies in a first aid kit:

- Sterile adhesive bandages in assorted sizes.
- Assorted sizes of safety pins.
- Cleansing agent/soap.
- Latex gloves (2 pair).
- 2-inch sterile gauze pads (4–6).
- 4-inch sterile gauze pads (4–6).
- Triangular bandages (3).
- Nonprescription drugs.
- 2-inch sterile roller bandages (3 rolls).
- 3-inch sterile roller bandages (3 rolls).
- Scissors.
- Tweezers.
- Moistened towelettes.
- Antiseptic.
- Thermometer.
- Tongue blades (2).
- Tube of petroleum jelly or other lubricant.

For minor cuts, rinse the affected area with cool running water and dry it with a clean towel or gauze. Apply an antiseptic and place a water-resistant bandage over the cut. If the cut is on the hand or fingers and the employee is returning to work, cover the hand with a plastic glove. For minor burns, place the burned area under cool running water or an ice pack. By definition, a minor burn is considered a first-degree burn, which is a reddening of the skin. In a second-degree burn, the affected area is blistered. In a third-degree burn, it is charred. In the case of second- and third-degree burns, immediate professional help should be sought.

The mere act of chewing and swallowing food can cause choking. While this is a rare occurrence, immediate action is necessary to prevent death. Key employees, at least one per shift, should be trained in the **Heimlich maneuver**. Again, courses are available from the Red Cross, local hospitals, community colleges, and others. Posters illustrating the Heimlich maneuver are available from the Red Cross.

Management should at all times stay calm during an emergency and maintain control of the situation. Keep the victim calm. Keep unnecessary people away from the area. If an emergency crew has been called, have a trusted employee meet them and direct them to the victim.

A written report is mandatory when an accident occurs. This is required by the Workmen's Compensation Program, by the operation's insurance company, and sometimes by the **Occupational Safety and Health Administration (OSHA)**. While the primary concern is the comfort and care of the victim once an accident has occurred, it is also important to fill out the report as soon as possible to avoid forgetting any pertinent facts.

When it comes to providing first aid to an employee or customer, take action immediately. While the purpose of this text is not to provide legal advice, it should be noted that by law, in practically every jurisdiction, a person cannot be held liable for taking action that would be taken by any other reasonable person in those circumstances. Consult a local attorney to make sure if this is the case in your area.

HAZARD COMMUNICATION STANDARD (HCS)

One of OSHA's mandates is the **Hazard Communication Standard (HCS)**. This mandate is predicated on the fact that employees have a right to know the hazards and identities of the chemicals they are working with. The manufacturers of these chemicals must evaluate the chemical hazards of their products and provide users with this information. In the foodservice industry, the manufacturer would provide the restaurant owner or the foodservice unit manager with the hazard data. The owner or manager would then communicate this to the employee.

To make sure that this communication is ongoing, every foodservice operation that is subject to OSHA regulations must have a handbook available in the kitchen that outlines each and every chemical in use in the kitchen. This handbook contains the **Material Safety Data Sheets (MSDS)** for each chemical that is in use in the kitchen. The MSDS lists the manufacturer's name and telephone number, the hazardous ingredients, the characteristics of those ingredients, fire and explosion data (if applicable), signs and symptoms of exposure, medical conditions caused by the exposure, emergency first aid procedures, disposal method if material is released or spilled, precautions to be taken, and control measures.

It is important to keep the book updated as chemical usage is changed. For example, if the dishwashing detergent is changed, the MSDS must be updated, since the chemical makeup of the new detergent could be different.

While this regulation applies only to larger operations that are under OSHA jurisdiction, it is a good idea for every foodservice operation to carry out this program. The MSDS are available to everyone, and the data to fill them out is obtainable from your supplier. A sample of an MSDS is shown in Figure 3.4. Should a chemical accident occur in your operation, the solution to the problem or the first aid to be administered has to be where you need it and when you need it.

Material Safety Data Sheet

May be used to comply with

OSHA's Hazard Communication Standard,
29 CFR 1910.1200. Standard must be
consulted for specific requirements.

U.S. Department of Labor

Occupational Safety and Health
Administration
(Non-Mandatory Form)
Form Approved
OMB No. 1218-0072

IDENTITY *(As Used on Label and List)*	Note: Blank spaces are not permitted. If any item is not applicable, or no information is available, the space must be marked to indicate that.

Section I

Manufacturer's Name	Emergency Telephone Number
Address *(Number, Street, City, State, and ZIP Code)*	Telephone Number for Information
	Date Prepared
	Signature of Preparer *(optional)*

Section II - Hazard Ingredients/Identity Information

Hazardous Components (Specific Chemical Identity; Common Name(s))	OSHA PEL	ACGIH TLV	Other Limits Recommended	%*(optional)*

FIGURE 3.4   A Material Safety Data Sheet (MSDS) that should be completed for each chemical used in the foodservice operation.

Source: Occupational Safety and Health Administration (OSHA).

Section III - Physical/Chemical Characteristics

Boiling Point		Specific Gravity (H_2O = 1)	
Vapor Pressure (mm Hg.)		Melting Point	
Vapor Density (AIR = 1)		Evaporation Rate (Butyl Acetate = 1)	
Solubility in Water			
Appearance and Odor			

Section IV - Fire and Explosion Hazard Data

Flash Point (Method Used)	Flammable Limits	LEL	UEL
Extinguishing Media			
Special Fire Fighting Procedures			
Unusual Fire and Explosion Hazards			

(Reproduce locally)   OSHA 174, Sept. 1985

FIGURE 3.4 (Continued)

Section V - Reactivity Data

Stability	Unstable		Conditions to Avoid
	Stable		
Incompatibility *(Materials to Avoid)*			
Hazardous Decomposition or Byproducts			
Hazardous Polymerization	May Occur		Conditions to Avoid
	Will Not Occur		

Section VI - Health Hazard Data

Route(s) of Entry:	Inhalation?	Skin?	Ingestion?
Health Hazards *(Acute and Chronic)*			
Carcinogenicity:	NTP?	IARC Monographs?	OSHA Regulated?
Signs and Symptoms of Exposure			
Medical Conditions Generally Aggravated by Exposure			
Emergency and First Aid Procedures			

FIGURE 3.4   (Continued)

Section VII - Precautions for Safe Handling and Use

Steps to Be Taken in Case Material is Released or Spilled
Waste Disposal Method
Precautions to Be taken in Handling and Storing
Other Precautions

Section VIII - Control Measures

Respiratory Proctection *(Specify Type)*		
Ventilation	Local Exhaust	Special
	Mechanical *(General)*	Other
Protective Gloves		Eye Protection
Other Protective Clothing or Equipment		
Work/Hygienic Practices		

Page 2   * U.S.G.P.O.: 1986 - 491 - 529/45775

FIGURE 3.4   (Continued)

CONCLUSION

The key is to be prepared. All employees need to be trained to know what to do in case of an emergency. This training needs to be practiced over and over in employee meetings. All too often, this is overlooked in the daily rush of preparing and serving meals. "It won't happen here" is no excuse. While accidents are rare, when they do happen, quick action is needed. There is no time to look in the book to see what to do.

Questions

1. You are a foodservice manager and the following events take place in your operation (hopefully not all on the same day). Tell what you would do in each instance. Be specific.

   A bartender takes a glass pitcher down from a shelf and drops it. The glass shatters and some of it lands in the condiment tray rack.
   A prep cook cuts his hand on the slicer and it is bleeding profusely.
   A delivery truck backs into the gas meter located immediately adjacent to your loading dock and knocks it loose, allowing gas to escape. Your restaurant is full of customers.
   Your sous chef runs into your office and tells you that the deep fryer has just caught on fire.

2. Distinguish between the four types of fires and tell why it is important to use the proper type of extinguisher on each.
3. What is OSHA? Why are MSDS important?
4. Why is knowing about carbon monoxide important?

Project

Find a restaurant in your neighborhood. Diagram it, showing all the exits, escape routes for employees and customers, and the locations of all the fire extinguishers. Conduct a training program for the management and employees of the restaurant on what to do in case of a fire.

Acknowledgments

The American Red Cross, Washington, DC.
United States Department of Labor, Occupational Safety and Health Administration, Washington, DC.

Web Sites

FDA Model Food Code
http://www.fda.gov

Occupational Safety and Health Administration (OSHA)
http://www.osha.gov

The American Red Cross
http://www.redcross.org

Resources

American Red Cross (2002). American Red Cross Community FirstAid and Safety. Washington, DC: American Red Cross.

Longree, K. & Armbruster, G. (1996). Quantity Food Sanitation, 5th ed. New York, NY: John Wiley & Sons, Inc.

National Assessment Institute (1998). Handbook for Safe Food Service Management, 2nd ed. Upper Saddle River, NJ: Prentice Hall.

National Restaurant Association Education Foundation (1999). Serve-Safe Coursebook. Chicago, IL: National Restaurant Association Education Foundation.

CHAPTER 4

Mechanical Equipment

Objectives

Upon completion of this chapter, you will be able to:

- Correctly disassemble, clean, reassemble, and operate a mixer, as well as operate the attachment hub.
- Demonstrate the proper procedure for operating a slicer and discuss the prevention of cross-contamination by using proper cleaning techniques.
- Describe the difference between a food cutter and a vertical cutter mixer and give applications for the use of each.
- Explain why a can opener is one of the major contributors of cross-contamination in the kitchen and how to correct the problem.

Key Terms

attachment hub	run, jog, and timer
belt-driven mixer	slicer automatic mode
buffalo chopper	slicer manual mode
gear-driven mixer	

In addition to these terms, the reader should also understand the terminology of the parts listed with each piece of equipment.

INTRODUCTION

Beginning with this chapter, we will look at many different pieces of equipment used in today's commercial kitchen. The equipment is grouped by categories, starting with mechanical equipment followed by cooking equipment, which, because of the large number of examples, is broken down into two chapters. Next is refrigeration, followed by sanitation equipment. Each section adheres to the following format:

- Overview—Tells about each piece of equipment, what it's used for, and its idiosyncrasies.
- Parts—Gives a description of the major parts making up that particular piece of equipment.
- Operation—Explains how the equipment is to be safely operated and any hazards to look out for.
- Disassembly—Goes over the proper procedure for taking the equipment apart for cleaning and maintenance.
- Cleaning—Covers what tools should be used to clean the equipment, the cleaning agents to be used, and the proper procedure to follow.
- Assembly—Explains how to put the equipment back together.
- Maintenance—What actions need to be taken to properly maintain the equipment so that it will perform to its full potential.

When reading these sections, keep two things in mind.

First, not everyone in the kitchen operates machinery correctly. The correct operating procedure is compiled from the major manufacturer's recommendations. They have researched, engineered, and built the equipment. They know its capabilities, limitations, and safety factors. Short-circuiting their recommendations is asking for trouble. For example, all manual slicers have a handle that the operator uses to guide the carriage back and forth. Yet, many operators put their hand on the product being sliced to move the carriage. This not only damages the carriage and the blade guard, but also sets up a dangerous situation where the operator's hand could easily slide into the slicer blade. By correctly operating the equipment, you will not only be protected by the built-in safety features but will also increase its longevity by not abusing it. As management, you must properly train your employees in the correct use of the equipment. By doing so, you will reduce accidents, increase productivity, and add to the life of the operation's capital investment.

Second, not all equipment is the same. Each manufacturer has different designs and different terminology. Sometimes these differences are slight and sometimes they are major. Even various models by the same manufacturer have differences. As technology improves, so does foodservice equipment. For these reasons, some of the explanations given in this text are generic in nature, especially in the "operation" section. The reader may notice subtle and, in rare cases, not so subtle differences between the explanations given and the actual equipment in use in their kitchens. For this reason, it is always wise to consult the operation manuals for the specific equipment in use.

MECHANICAL EQUIPMENT

Mechanical equipment, for the most part, is powered by electricity. It allows the user to produce large volumes of product in a short period of time. Equipment covered in this section includes slicers, mixers, vertical cutter mixers, food choppers, food processors, and can openers. Consider the amount of time saved by blending batter for 30 dozen cupcakes by hand rather than in a mixer, slicing 100 tomatoes by hand than on a slicer, or preparing 350 portions of coleslaw by hand rather than in a VCM (vertical cutter mixer). High-volume food service is possible because of these tools. Mechanical equipment must be meticulously cleaned and sanitized after each use since this group, more than any other, has the potential for cross-contamination.

MIXER

Overview

The mixer is one of the workhorses of the kitchen. Its primary purpose is to blend products such as batter, dough, salad dressings, or whipping cream. Because of its versatility, it comes with several attachments, called agitators, that perform the various functions. This feature, coupled with three or more speeds, gives the mixer a diverse base to perform a wide range of functions. Many mixers are equipped with an **attachment hub** that, in addition to the above duties, permits them to grind meat, slice vegetables, grate vegetables and cheese, and rasp breadcrumbs (see Figure 4.1).

Mixers are either gear-driven or belt-driven. In the case of a **gear-driven mixer**, the agitator is turned by a series of gears powered by the motor. In a **belt-driven mixer**, the agitator is turned by a belt powered by the motor. This works on the same principle as the fan belt in your car. While important in the design of the machine, whether it is gear- or belt-driven is of little consequence in the operation of the mixer.

FIGURE 4.1

Source: Hobart.

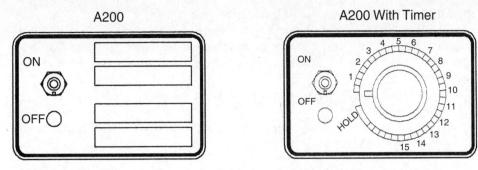

FIGURE 4.2 On the left side is a power switch without a timer and on the right side is a power switch with a timer.

Source: Hobart.

Parts

Power switch—Used to turn the mixer either on or off.

Timer (not available on all models)—Allows the operator to set the amount of time the mixer should run. When the time on the timer elapses, the mixer shuts off. To allow the mixer to run until it is manually shut off, set the timer to HOLD (see Figure 4.2).

Gearshift lever—(see Figure 4.3) Allows the operator to select the speed at which the mixer will operate. While most mixers have three speeds, some are equipped with up to nine speeds. When it is necessary to change speeds during the mixing process, always turn the power switch to the OFF position before changing gears. Those with three speeds should be used as follows:

- Speed 1 or Low—Used for heavy mixtures such as bread dough, heavy batter, and whipping potatoes.
- Speed 2 or Medium—Used for quick rise light dough, batter, and some whipping operations.
- Speed 3 or High—Used for light work such as whipping cream, beating eggs or egg whites, and mixing thin batters.

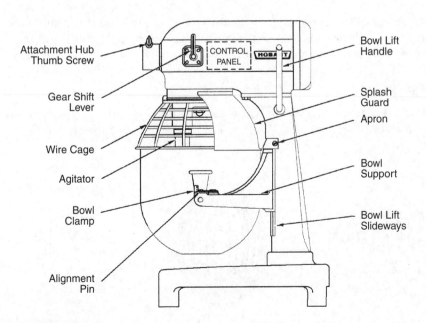

FIGURE 4.3 Mixer parts.

Source: Hobart.

Bowl lift handle—Used to raise or lower the bowl.

Bowl guard (newer models only)—Prevents users from putting their hands and/or utensils in the bowl while the machine is on. The bowl guard uses an interlock system that prevents the mixer from running unless the guard is locked in place.

Agitators—Most mixers are supplied with three agitators: a flat beater, a wire whip, and a dough hook. Three additional agitators can be procured at an extra cost; they include a wing whip, a pastry knife, and a heavy-duty whip. The agitators are as follows:

- Flat beater—A multipurpose agitator used for the uniform dispersion of ingredients and products requiring a creaming or a rubbing action. Also used for mixing ingredients such as cake batter, icing, and mashed potatoes. The first (low) speed is normally used for starting the mixing operation and the second (medium) speed for finishing it (see Figure 4.4).
- Wire whip—An agitator that is used to blend air into light products. Used primarily for whipping cream, beating eggs, light icings, and meringues. Normally used in second (medium) and third (high) speeds (see Figure 4.5).
- Dough hooks—The agitator used for mixing yeast-raised dough that requires folding and stretching. Examples include bread, roll, and pizza dough. Dough hooks should be operated on the first (low) or second (medium) speed (see Figure 4.6).
- Wing whip—A version of the wire whip that has four or six wings depending on the size of the mixer. Used to cream or beat ingredients that are too heavy for the wire whip such as whipping butter or mayonnaise. Can also be used to whip potatoes or icings (see Figure 4.7).
- Pastry knife—Used to combine flour with shortening, allowing delicate ingredients to be combined without over-development, for example, pie dough and pastry shells. The pastry knife should be used at the first (low) or second (medium) speed. Third (high) speed will result in a pastry without a flaky texture (see Figure 4.8).
- Heavy-duty whip—An industrial version of the wire whip that is used to whip heavier ingredients, such as sponge cake or marshmallow (see Figure 4.9).

ATTACHMENTS If the mixer is gear-driven, you can use three hub attachments: the meat grinder attachment, the vegetable slicer attachment, and the grating/shredding attachment (see Figure 4.10).

Operation

If you are using an older mixer without a bowl guard, remember to keep your hands, clothing, and utensils out of the bowl while the mixer is running.

FIGURE 4.4 Flat beater.

Source: Hobart.

FIGURE 4.5 Wire whip.

Source: Hobart.

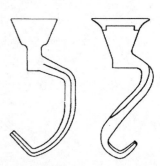

FIGURE 4.6 Dough hook.

Source: Hobart.

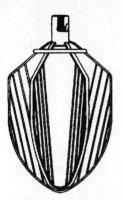

FIGURE 4.7 Wing whip.
Source: Hobart.

FIGURE 4.8 Pastry knife.
Source: Hobart.

FIGURE 4.9 Heavy duty whip.
Source: Hobart.

To operate the mixer:

- Install the bowl. Lower the bowl support all the way. Position the bowl so that the alignment bracket (pin) on the back of the bowl fits into the bowl retainer on the mixer. Line up the holes on the bracket on the sides of the bowl with the pins on the sides of the bowl support. Lock the bowl in place by rotating the bowl clamps over the pins going through the holes. *Note*: Some models require that the agitator be placed in the bowl prior to installing the bowl.
- Install the agitator. Select the correct agitator (beater, whip, or dough hook) for the job. Place the agitator in the bowl. Align it with the pin and push it up on the agitator shaft. Turn it clockwise until the shaft pin is seated in the slot of the agitator shank.
- Place the product or ingredients to be mixed into the bowl.
- Raise the bowl using the bowl lift handle.
- Close the wire cage assembly (if the mixer is so equipped).
- Select the speed at which you wish to mix. If it is necessary to change speeds during the mixing process, the power switch must be turned to the OFF position prior to changing gears.
- Turn the power switch to ON.
- Some recipes require that the bowl be raised during the mixing process. If this is the case, use the low speed (1). Hold the power switch in the upper-most position with one hand and raise the bowl with the bowl lift handle with the other hand.

FIGURE 4.10 On the left is a grinding attachment and on the right is the housing for the slicing and shredding blade attachments.
Source: Hobart.

Disassembly

Three pieces should be removed and cleaned on a periodic basis (at least weekly): the wire cage assembly, the splashguard, and the apron.

To remove the wire cage assembly:

- Lower the bowl and rotate the wire cage to the left until it is positioned underneath the splashguard (see Figure 4.11).
- Remove the agitator and bowl.
- Hold the wire cage assembly with both hands and rotate it completely to the left. When the front-center retainer (the white thing) reaches the end of its travel, it can be lowered through the flat on the drip cup ridge.
- After lowering the retainer, move the wire cage assembly to the rear so that the three rear retainers (the white things) clear the drip cup ridge.
- The wire cage assembly can now be lowered and removed.

To take the splashguard off, unscrew the three screws and remove it. Likewise the apron can be removed by loosening the two screws that hold it on.

Cleaning

The mixer, agitator, bowl, or attachments should be cleaned after each use. Prior to cleaning the mixer, make sure the power switch is in the OFF position and unplug the power cord.

- Mixer bowls, agitators, and the wire cage can be cleaned and sanitized in a pot and pan sink using hot water and a mild detergent solution, or they can be washed in the dish machine. Thoroughly rinse after washing.
- The mixer itself can be cleaned with a damp cloth that has been immersed in a solution of hot water and mild detergent. Never use a hose. When cleaning the mixer, make sure to wipe down the underside of the motor housing since product has a tendency to splash up and hit the base.
- Periodically, weekly at the very least, the wire cage, apron, and bowl splashguard should be removed by detaching the screws and cleaned in a sink or dish machine.

Assembly

Reassemble the three parts that were removed, namely the wire cage assembly, the splashguard, and the apron.

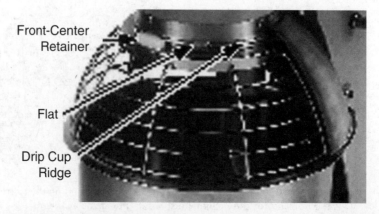

Front-Center Retainer

Flat

Drip Cup Ridge

FIGURE 4.11   Mixer guard parts.

Source: Hobart.

To reattach the wire cage:

- Hold it so that its top ring is positioned around the drip cup. The grooves in the rear retainers (the white things) should straddle the ridge on the drip cup.
- Lift the assembly so that the front retainer (the white thing) passes up and through the flat on the ridge of the drip cup.
- Rotate the wire cage assembly to the right until all three retainers straddle the ridge on the drip cup in the three opposed locations.
- Rotate the wire cage assembly to the right until it stops at its front-center position.
- Reattach the splashguard and the apron by placing them in their proper respective positions and tighten the screws.

Maintenance

The primary maintenance to be performed on the mixer is lubrication. Monthly, when the apron is off for cleaning, apply a light coat of lubricant to the three sides of the two slideways. Twice a year, lubricate the bowl clamps.

SLICER

Overview

The slicer is one of the most dangerous pieces of equipment in the kitchen. This applies not only to its operation but also to the assembling, disassembling, and cleaning process. It is imperative that employees are trained in the proper use and maintenance of this piece of equipment. While most manufacturers have designed their slicers with built-in safety devices, the employee must utilize them in order for them to be effective.

When purchasing a slicer, choose one that has a minimum of removable parts. This will make it easier to clean and sanitize, and you won't have to hire employees with a Ph.D. in mechanical engineering to disassemble and assemble it. The base and sides should be coved, not at right angles, for easier cleaning and to avoid food getting into crevices. The knife blade should be completely covered with a blade guard to prevent employees from touching the blade while the slicer is running (see Figure 4.12).

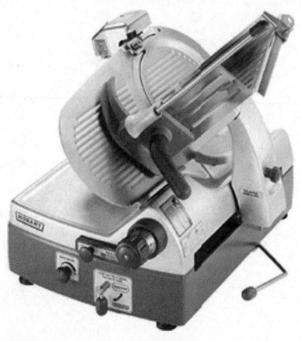

FIGURE 4.12

Source: Hobart.

Parts

Carriage tray—The piece that holds the product to be sliced.

Meat grip (sometimes called a holder)—A piece that holds the product firmly in place on the carriage tray and pushes it into the gauge plate.

Fence—An adjustable piece that narrows the width of the carriage tray in order to hold the product being sliced more securely to the tray. *Note*: Not all slicers come equipped with a fence.

Knife blade—The part that slices the product by rotating at a high rate of RPM (rotations per minute).

Knife cover—The metal piece at the top of the knife blade that prevents the user from touching the blade while the machine is running.

Carriage tray handle—The device used to move the carriage tray back and forth.

Gauge plate—The piece that the product rests on as the meat grip pushes it down the carriage. The index knob moves the gauge plate, thus determining how thick the product will be sliced.

Index knob—The dial that moves the gauge plate to determine the thickness of slice. Be aware that the numbers on the knob have no relevance to actual measurements, such as number of slices per inch or centimeter; they are merely used as reference points.

Switch—Turns the slicer on and off (see Figure 4.13).

Operation

Regarding the operation of slicers, there are two different types: manual and automatic. A manual slicer is operated by the carriage being moved back and forth by the operator. With an automatic slicer, the carriage is moved back and forth mechanically.

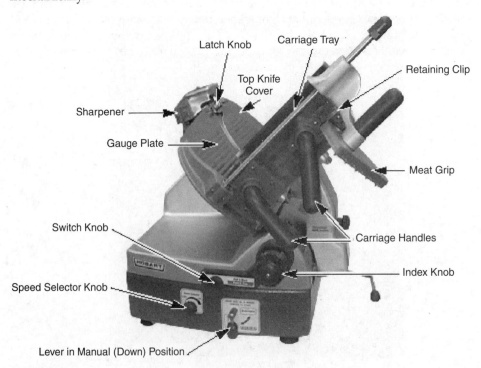

FIGURE 4.13

Source: Hobart.

MANUAL MODE

- Make sure the index knob is on zero, which will completely close the gauge plate.
- Pull the carriage toward you until it stops.
- Place the product to be sliced on the carriage tray. If the meat grip is to be used to securely hold the product, swing it around and place it against the product. It is strongly advised to use the meat grip whenever possible.
- Turn the index knob to select the desired thickness of cut.
- Turn the slicer on by pulling or flipping the switch knob to the ON position.
- Using the carriage tray handle, push the carriage back and forth to slice the product. Never push the carriage by placing your hand on the product being sliced and moving it back and forth. Many cooks do this and countless serious accidents are needlessly caused by this improper action.

AUTOMATIC MODE

- Place the product on the carriage. If the fence is to be used, loosen the thumbscrew and push the fence to the product, but not firmly against it. Tighten the thumbscrew.
- Place the meat grip on the product and push the carriage all the way forward.
- Select the thickness of slice by turning the index knob.
- On the front of most machines is a lever for operating the slicer in a manual mode or an automatic mode. Make sure the lever is in the manual mode.
- Also on the front is the speed selector knob. Using this, select the speed at which you wish the slicer to operate.
- Turn the slicer ON.
- Turn the lever from the manual position to the automatic position. The slicer will now slice the product at the thickness and speed you have indicated.
- To stop the unit, turn the lever to the manual position and turn the slicer to the OFF position.

Disassembly

To disassemble the slicer for cleaning purposes:

- Make sure the slicer is turned to the OFF position.
- Unplug the power cord.
- Turn the index knob clockwise to zero to close the gauge plate against the knife blade, reducing the risk of accidentally coming into contact with the blade.
- Remove the carriage tray by unscrewing the knob at the base of the tray and, with both hands, lift the carriage tray straight up.
- Remove the top knife cover.
- Remove the deflector, which is located beneath the slicer blade.

Cleaning

The slicer should be thoroughly cleaned and sanitized after each use. In reality, many operations do not do this, waiting to the end of the shift to do the heavy cleaning. This is not, however, a very good idea because, with different products being sliced, cross-contamination could easily occur. To prevent this from happening in your operation, clean it after each use. Always make sure that the slicer is unplugged prior to the cleaning process.

- Wash the carriage tray, knife cover, deflector, and the sharpener in the pot and pan sink and sanitize using a chlorinated sanitizing solution. *Note*: Most manufacturers recommend against washing slicer parts in the dishwasher.
- Wipe off all surfaces of the slicer using a clean cloth, which has been soaked in warm water and a mild detergent.
- Rinse using a fresh cloth soaked in clean water.
- With a folded paper towel, clean between the ring guard and knife blade. Insert the folded paper towel at the base of the ring guard and manually rotate the knife blade. This will clean the ring guard and the edge of the gauge plate as it follows the knife around (see Figure 4.14).
- Wash and rinse both sides of the blade by wiping from the center of the blade outward.

Note: Some slicers come equipped with a cleaning leg that is located under the base of the slicer. To engage the cleaning leg, lift the front of the slicer up and the leg will drop down. Pull the leg forward until it is engaged and completely supporting the slicer (see Figure 4.15).
Now for some "do nots":

- Do not use steel pads on any part of the slicer.
- Do not exceed the manufacturer's recommended concentrations for detergent or sanitizer, because it will corrode the metal.
- Do not wash slicer parts in a dishwasher; the heavy-duty detergent will, again, corrode the metal.
- Do not immerse the slicer base or motor in water.
- Do not hose down the slicer.

Assembly

To reassemble the slicer:

- Replace the sharpener, if the slicer is equipped with one. *Note*: Make sure the sharpener is engaged securely.
- Replace the top knife cover.
- Replace the deflector below the knife blade.
- Take the carriage tray and, holding it with both hands, lower it so that the key on the bottom fits into the slot on the carriage pivot. Tilt the carriage tray to the left and secure it by turning the knob on the carriage tray support arm until it is snug.

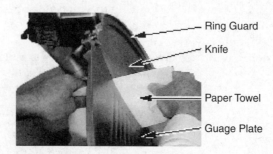

Ring Guard

Knife

Paper Towel

Guage Plate

FIGURE 4.14

Source: Hobart.

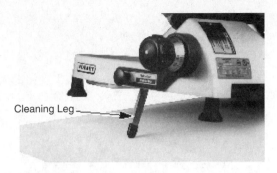

Cleaning Leg

FIGURE 4.15

Source: Hobart.

Maintenance

KNIFE SHARPENING   A sharp blade is essential in getting a clean cut on your product. A dull blade will rip or tear the food, which will result in a poor looking product, increased waste, and ultimately an increased food cost. On the other hand, if the knife blade is sharpened too frequently, excessive wear will occur and the blade will have to be replaced soon. While there is no set rule of thumb on how often the blade should be sharpened, common sense should prevail. In an operation where there is a heavy usage, such as a high-volume deli, it should be done daily. Moderate use would require weekly sharpening and an operation with low use, monthly. In the interest of serving a good-looking product and reducing food cost, it would be best to err on the side of sharpening too often.

To sharpen the knife blade (see Figure 4.16):

- Unplug the power cord.
- Turn the index knob to zero, closing the gauge plate.
- Remove the knife cover by turning the latch knob counterclockwise and lifting it off the slicer.
- Wipe off the exposed knife surface and the area surrounding the knife blade. Make sure it is totally clean and free from any fat residue.
- On most slicers, the sharpening device is attached to the top of the slicer. If the model you are using has a detached sharpener, attach it by slipping the

To Sharpen
Pull Sharpener Handle
Fully Forward
For 5 Seconds

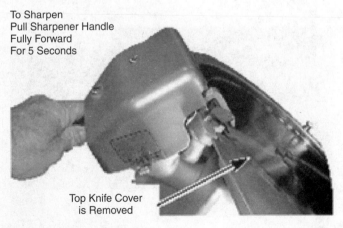

Top Knife Cover
is Removed

FIGURE 4.16   Sharpening the slicer.

Source: Hobart.

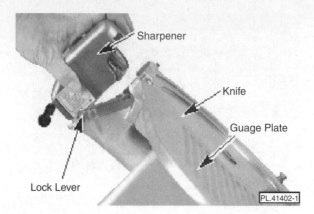

FIGURE 4.17 Assembling a detached sharpening device.
Source: Hobart.

sharpener into the groove and turning the wing nut (lock lever) clockwise to lock it (see Figure 4.17).

- Plug in the power cord.
- Turn the slicer on.
- Pull the knob on the sharpening device toward you for five seconds and release.
- Turn the slicer off.
- Unplug the power cord.
- Using a clean damp cloth, wipe off the blade to remove any grinding particles.

LUBRICATION The carriage slide rod should be lubricated monthly. To do this, apply four to five drops of the lubricating oil onto the carriage slide rod located on the underside of the slicer. After applying the oil, move the carriage tray back and forth several times to properly distribute the oil (see Figure 4.18).

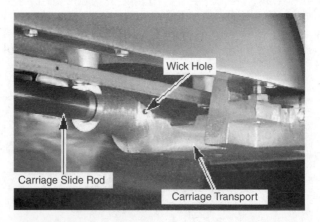

FIGURE 4.18 Carriage slide lubrication.
Source: Hobart.

CUTTER MIXERS

Overview

Cutter mixers, often called VCMs, are among the more versatile machines in the kitchen. For the most part, they can pretty much do on a large scale what a food processor can do on a small scale. They can cut vegetables, cheese, and meat

FIGURE 4.19
Source: Hobart.

products. They can blend products such as meat loaf and salad dressings. They can mix batters and knead yeast dough. And they do all of this very quickly. In most cases, it will take longer to clean the cutter mixer than it will for the machine to do its work (see Figure 4.19).

Like other kitchen equipment, it is potentially dangerous. However, if it is used correctly, it is safe. It has an electromechanical interlock that prevents the machine from being turned on if the lid is not properly locked in place. Also, the lid cannot be raised during operation without the machine being shut off.

Parts

START switch—Starts the cutter mixer when depressed.

STOP switch—Stops the cutter mixer when depressed.

Timer—Has three settings: **run, jog, and timer**.

Run—The machine runs continuously when the START switch is depressed and continues running until the STOP switch is depressed.

Jog—The machine runs while the START switch is held down and stops when it is released. Works similar to the pulse command on a food processor.

Timer—The machine runs for the specified amount of time set on the timer. When the time elapses, the machine shuts off. The maximum time is five minutes.

Mixing baffle—A hand-operated attachment that allows the user to stir the product in the bowl while it is being cut or mixed (see Figure 4.20). Also allows the user to push the product into the knives.

Lid latch—Locks the lid into place. Has an electromechanical interlock that prevents the machine from running unless the lid is locked.

Bowl tilt handle—Allows for the tilting and emptying of the bowl. When the bowl tilt handle is pushed down, the bowl tilts forward. When it is lifted, the bowl reverts to its original position.

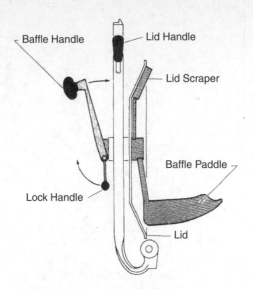

FIGURE 4.20 Cutter mixer parts.

Source: Hobart.

Cut mix assembly—An attachment that cuts produce, meat, and cheese. Also used for batters and doughs that need to be cut and mixed.

Knead mix assembly—Used where cutting is not needed, such as blending and mixing products as well as kneading yeast dough.

Strainer basket—An attachment used when cutting vegetables in water (see Figure 4.21).

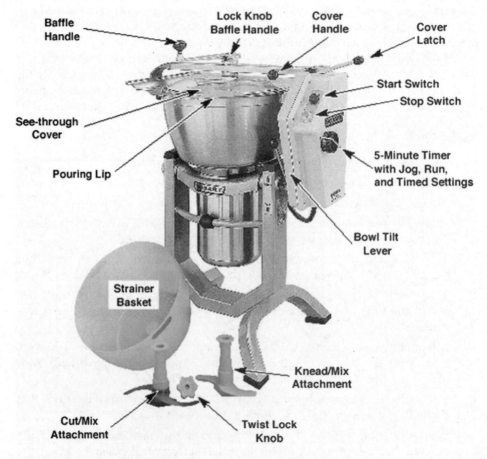

FIGURE 4.21 Parts of a mixing baffle.

Source: Hobart.

Operation

To safely operate the cutter mixer:

- Move the bowl tilt handle to HOLD to lock the bowl in a vertical position.
- If the strainer basket is to be used, place it in the bowl.
- Select the cut mix assembly or the knead mix assembly and attach it.
- Attach the mixing baffle if it is to be used.
- Place product to be processed into the bowl. If the strainer basket is used, add water.
- Close the lid. Press the lid down with the lid handle while turning the lid latch until it is engaged.
- Set the timer to RUN, JOG, or TIMER. (See the "Parts" section for the proper setting.)
- Turn the machine on.
- When the product is processed, turn the machine off.
- After the shaft has stopped, open the cover by releasing the lid latch.
- Remove the cut mix assembly. If the knead mix assembly was used, it can remain in place.
- If necessary, scrape the lid.
- If the strainer basket was used, lift it out and allow the water to drain through the holes in the bottom of the basket.
- Move the bowl tilt handle to TILT
- Grasp the lid handle and pull the bowl toward you slowly, emptying the contents of the bowl into a container.
- Return the bowl to its upright and vertical position.
- Return the bowl tilt handle to the HOLD position.
- If another load of identical product is to be processed, do so at this time.
- If a load of a different product is to be processed, the machine must be cleaned and sanitized first to avoid cross-contamination.
- If processing is complete, clean the machine at this time.

Cleaning

Because several materials are used in the construction of the cutter mixer, that is, plastic, metal, and stainless steel, certain cleaning materials should not be used. Do not use any harsh abrasives, steel wool or other abrasive pads, cleaners containing ammonia or chlorine, window sprays, chemical adhesives, drain cleaners, or commercial dishwasher detergents.

Prior to cleaning the cutter mixer, prewash it by pouring 1 gallon of warm water into the bowl along with one or two tablespoons of a mild liquid household detergent. Replace the cut mix or knead mix assembly. Close and latch the lid and jog the machine for three bursts of three seconds each. Leave the soapy water in the bowl. The unit is now ready for cleaning.

- Unplug the unit.
- Remove the cut mix or knead mix assembly and the mixing baffle (if used).
- Hand wash, rinse, and sanitize the attachments in the pot and pan sink.
- Wash the inside of the bowl and the underside of the lid with a cloth or sponge. Use a plastic spatula to scrape any product that adheres to the side of the bowl.
- Tilt the unit forward and empty the bowl.
- Pour 1 gallon of warm water into the bowl and rinse the underside of the lid and the bowl.
- Tilt the unit forward and empty the bowl.
- Let the bowl air dry.
- Remove the bowl seal by lifting it up and off the motor shaft.
- Separate the seal from the retainer.

- In the pot and pan sink, wash, rinse, and sanitize the seal and retainer.
- Reassemble the seal and retainer and reinstall them, making sure that the thin black edge is down and the white-tapered part is up. Push the seal down firmly over the shaft and twist it to seal it against the bottom of the bowl.

Put the cut mix assembly, the knead mix assembly, the mixing baffle, and the strainer basket on a shelf. Do not leave them in the cutter mixer for storage. Also leave the lid unattached when the machine is not in use.

Maintenance

The motor bearings are prelubricated and should be checked by a service technician every three years. No other maintenance is required.

FOOD CUTTER

Overview

Food cutters are also known in the foodservice industry as food choppers and **buffalo choppers** (don't ask why, I don't know). It is quite a useful piece of equipment for chopping foods such as celery, onions, cabbage, or potatoes, as well as meat and other products. It is often used to make breadcrumbs and is also used in the garde-manger kitchen to make sausage (see Figure 4.22).

The food cutter has a rotating bowl. A cover fits over the bowl. On the underside of the cover is a plow formation that guides the product in the bowl under two power-driven knives. As the bowl is rotating with the product in it, the knives are turning, thus cutting or chopping the food. The longer the product is left in the rotating bowl, the finer the cut becomes.

If the food cutter is used correctly, it is a very safe machine. The cover is fitted with a locking device that must be in place before the machine will turn

FIGURE 4.22
Source: Hobart.

on. Thus, the knives will not turn until the lid is securely locked in place. The plow formation that is located under the lid to guide the food into the knives also helps prevent a hand from going under the lid and into the knives. Given all these safety features, it is still possible to have your hand come into contact with the knives; therefore when operating this machine, always keep your hands away from the bowl and cover. Use a spatula to remove product from the bowl.

Some food cutters have a hub attachment that allows you to use the same attachments that are used on the mixer hub. Thus, a dual use can be made of attachments. To do this, both the mixer and the food cutter must be from the same manufacturer.

Parts

START/STOP switch—The switch that turns the food cutter on and off. (see Figure 4.23)

Bowl—The receptacle where food is placed to be cut or chopped. The bowl rotates and the food passes under two rotating knives.

Bowl cover—A lid over the bowl containing the plow formation that guides the food into the knife blades. (see Figure 4.23)

Locking handle—A device that locks the bowl cover into place over the bowl. The machine will not start until the bowl cover is in place and the locking handle is turned. (see Figure 4.23)

Comb—A plate with two grooves that sits between the blades to keep them clean as they rotate. (see Figure 4.24)

Hand knob—A handle that turns to tighten the knives and keep them in place. (see Figure 4.24)

Hub attachment plug—The place where the attachments are hooked on to the food cutter. (Not available on all machines.)

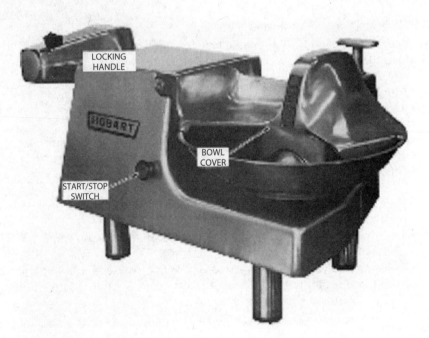

FIGURE 4.23 Food cutter parts.

Source: Hobart.

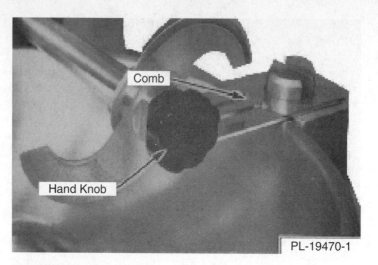

FIGURE 4.24 Blade and comb assembly.
Source: Hobart.

Operation

- To start the food cutter, pull out the START/STOP switch. At this point, the bowl will go around and the knives will rotate (see Figure 4.24). Place the product to be cut, chopped, or ground into the bowl. As the product goes around in the bowl, it will be processed.
- When it reaches the desired consistency, remove the product from the bowl using a rubber spatula. The food cutter can be either in the ON or OFF position when removing product. If it is in the ON position, be careful not to place your hand or the spatula under the bowl cover.
- To stop the food cutter, push the START/STOP switch in. Again, do not place your hands under the bowl cover while the machine is running.

Cleaning

The exterior of the food cutter should be wiped daily with a clean damp cloth. The interior and parts should be cleaned and sanitized after each use. To do this:

- Unplug the food cutter.
- Unlock and raise the bowl cover.
- Remove the comb.
- Turn the knife shaft so that the knives are in a horizontal position.
- Remove the hand knob on the knife shaft.
- Slide the knife unit off of the shaft. The knives are sharp. Use extreme caution.
- Remove the bowl by rotating it clockwise and lifting if from the bowl support.
- In the pot and pan sink, wash, rinse, and sanitize the bowl, knife, hand knob, and comb.
- Reassemble the parts in reverse order. When reassembling the knife, make sure that the slot in the knife hub is mated to the notch in the knife shaft. Tighten the hand knob securely.

Maintenance

The motor requires no lubrication. As needed, the knives should be sharpened using an ordinary sharpening stone.

FIGURE 4.25
Source: Edlund.

COMMERCIAL CAN OPENER

Overview

One of the smallest pieces of equipment in the kitchen, the can opener can create havoc with food safety because it's not cleaned often enough (see Figure 4.25). When the can opener is used, food gets trapped between the blade and the opener assembly. It sits there at room temperature growing bacteria and then contaminates the next product being opened. The can opener should be washed after each use. Another problem occurs when the blade becomes dull and creates a groove, which creates metal shavings that end up in the food. For these reasons, you can count on the health department inspecting the can opener during an inspection.

Parts

There are three operating parts in the commercial can opener:

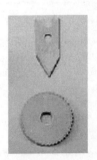

FIGURE 4.26 Top: A can opener blade. Bottom: A can opener gear assembly.

Source: Edlund.

- The handle—The part that is turned to allow the blade to open the can.
- Gear—The piece that transforms the turning of the handle to the turning of the can to be opened.
- Blade—The part that cuts the can lid open (see Figure 4.26).

Operation

Lift the handle straight up, perpendicular to the table top and high enough so that the can fits under the blade. Place the can under the handle and blade. Push down on the handle so that the blade punctures the top of the can lid. Lower the handle so that it is parallel to the tabletop. Turn the handle, which will turn the can while the blade opens the can top.

Disassembly

The only part that needs to be removed is the blade. This is done by pulling a pin on the cutting side of the opener and removing the blade. On some models instead of a pin, there are two screws that need to be removed to release the blade. The only time the blade is removed is either to replace it or to remove a piece of food. This occasionally happens when some food gets lodged between the blade and the opener shaft that was not removed during the washing cycle.

Cleaning

Remove the opener from the worktable and run it through the dishwasher. It's just that simple. After washing, check the gear, the blade, and the can opener shaft to make sure that there are no particles of food that were not washed away during the dishwashing cycle.

Assembly

Replace the blade by pulling the pin, place the blade behind the pin assembly, and release the pin. The blade should now be securely in place. If the model uses screws, place the blade behind the blade cover and tighten the two screws.

Maintenance

There are two maintenance functions required on a commercial can opener. First is replacing the blade. Every time the can opener is washed, the blade should be checked for wear. Over time, a small groove will develop in the blade and at this time it should be replaced. Many blades are reversible thus doubling their life. Caution: Don't reverse an old blade that has a groove on both sides. The groove in the blade creates metal shavings from the can lid. These shavings could easily end up in the food and cause injury to your customer.

The second maintenance function is to replace the gear should it become worn. While this is a relatively simple procedure, follow the manufacturer's directions as the procedure is different depending on the make and model.

Questions

1. Explain the attachment hub on a mixer and give several examples of its application.
2. Identify the following agitators and tell what each is used for.
3. Discuss the relationship between a slicer's construction and its safe operation.
4. Tell when a slicer should be cleaned and why it's important to clean it at that time.
5. Explain run, jog, and timer on a vertical cutter mixer.
6. List and explain the safety features on a food cutter.

Project

With other members of your class, take turns demonstrating and explaining how to disassemble, clean, and assemble a mixer, slicer, vertical cutter mixer, food cutter, and can opener.

Acknowledgments

Edlund Company Inc., Burlington VT.
Globe Food Equipment, Dayton OH.

Hobart Corporation, Troy OH.

Web Sites

Berkel Incorporated
www.averyberkel.com

Edlund Company Inc.
www.edlundco.com

General Slicing
www.generalslicing.com

Globe Food Equipment
www.globeslicers.com

Hobart Corporation
www.hobartcorp.com

Univex
www.univexcorp.com

Resources

Birchfield, John C. (1998). Design and Layout of Foodservice Facilities. New York, NY: John Wiley & Sons, Inc.

Katsigris, Costas & Thomas, Chris (1999). Design and Equipment for Restaurants and Food-service: A Management View. New York, NY: John Wiley & Sons, Inc.

Kazarian, Edward A. (1997). Foodservice Facilities Planning, 3rd ed. New York, NY: John Wiley & Sons, Inc.

Scriven, C. & Stevens, J. (1982). Food Equipment Facts. New York, NY: John Wiley & Sons, Inc.

Product specification sheets and owners manual from the following companies:

Berkel Inc.
Edlund Company Inc.
Globe Food Equipment Inc.
Hobart Corporation
Univex Corporation

CHAPTER 5

Cooking Equipment Part I

Objectives

Upon completion of this chapter, you will be able to:

- Explain how a thermostat operates to control the temperature of a cooking appliance.
- Discuss the operational difference between a gas and an electric burner control knob.
- Explain how a gas spark ignition system works to light the pilot light.
- Demonstrate how to light a standing gas pilot light.
- Differentiate between the various types of range tops and tell the use of each.
- Explain how induction cooking is different from the traditional gas and electric cooktops.
- Demonstrate how to clean a deep fat fryer.
- Discuss the different types of griddle tops and how to clean each of them.
- Tell why a proofing cabinet is an integral part of the baking process.
- Differentiate between an urn and decanter brewing process and describe the application of each.

Key Terms

BTU
burner control knob
cal rod
French plate
open burner

proofing process
spark ignition
standing pilot light
solid surface (flat top)
thermostat

INTRODUCTION

Cooking equipment constitutes such a large group that this section has been broken down into two chapters: Cooking Equipment Part I and Cooking Equipment Part II.

Cooking equipment for the most part is fueled by either gas or electricity. Some exceptions are an open flame grill or broiler that could be fueled by either wood or charcoal. Another exception is steam equipment that receives its steam from a central boiler, as opposed to being self-generated. (Self-generated steam is fueled by either electricity or gas.)

THERMOSTAT

Regardless of the power source, some generalities cover all cooking equipment. First and foremost is the control of temperature. Either a thermostat or a burner control knob manages this function.

On equipment that uses a thermostat, such as an oven, the thermostat is set to the desired temperature. The equipment is turned on and, if it is operated by gas, an automatic valve admits gas to the heating element where it is ignited by a flame. The lit gas flows through the heating element at full capacity. If it is electric, the power goes to the heating element and heats that element at full capacity. When the desired temperature is reached, the thermostat shuts off the gas or electrical flow. In other words, the amount of gas or electrical energy is not regulated—it's either on at full capacity or it's off. When the unit (oven) starts cooling off due to lack of a heat source, the thermostat opens the flow of gas or electrical power until the desired temperature is again reached. The process is repeated as the temperature in the equipment ebbs and flows. The unit operates in an "all-or-nothing" manner. Turning the thermostat to a higher temperature will not increase the gas flow or the electrical power, it will merely increase the amount of time that the gas flows through the burner or the electricity heats the heating element. In other words, the unit will not heat quicker with a higher temperature setting; it will only stay on longer.

BURNER CONTROL KNOB

The temperature on the top of the range is controlled by **burner control knobs** that operate differently depending on whether gas or electricity is being used. On gas equipment that uses a burner control knob, a stove for example, the amount of gas going into the unit is controlled. When the knob is set on low, a smaller amount of gas is going into the burner and the flame is low with fewer BTUs (British thermal units), which measure heat intensity.

When the knob is set on high, a greater amount of gas enters the burner, resulting in a higher flame and a larger number of BTUs. Thus, with a gas burner control knob, the amount of gas controls the temperature.

An electrical burner control knob operates in the same way that a thermostat operates. It pulsates on and off to control the temperature of the burner. If the burner is turned to low, the heating element goes on at full power. When the low temperature is reached, the power goes off. As the burner cools down, the power comes on, and it again goes off when the low temperature is reached. With an electrical burner control knob, it is the time that the power is on that controls temperature, unlike a gas burner control knob, which controls temperature with the amount of gas.

GAS PILOT LIGHTS

When an electrical cooking appliance is turned on, the power goes straight to the heating element and the heating process begins. Gas equipment cooks by means of a hot flame that comes from a burner. As gas flows into the burner, it needs to be ignited to produce a flame. To achieve this, the unit is equipped with either a spark ignition system or a pilot light. Either of these systems produces the flame that ignites the gas.

With the electronic **spark ignition**, when the burner control knob or the power switch to the equipment is turned on, it starts the spark igniter and at the same time opens the gas valve for the pilot light. The spark ignites the gas, thus lighting the pilot flame. The pilot flame then heats up the sensor, and the sensor sends a signal to turn off the spark. The pilot flame stays lit as long as the burner is on or the power switch to the equipment is on.

When either one of these is turned off, the pilot flame goes out. The process must be repeated for the pilot light to be relit. On units where the temperature is controlled by a thermostat and the unit goes on and off to maintain the heat level, the pilot flame will stay lit as long as the power switch is in the ON position. The electronic spark ignition is the most economical system because it conserves gas and reduces heat in the kitchen when the unit is off.

A **standing pilot light** is different, in that, once the pilot flame is lit, it stays on whether the equipment is on or off. The only time the flame goes out is when there is an interruption of the gas service going to the piece of equipment or if there is a malfunction. The standing pilot ignition must be lit manually. To light (or relight) the pilot flame:

- Make sure the gas supply valve to the equipment is open.
- Turn the thermostat control knob on the equipment counterclockwise to the OFF position.
- Push the pilot control knob in and turn it to the ON position and continue to push it in.
- Using a long match or a hand-held propane starter, hold a flame to the pilot light orifice until the pilot light ignites. Do not use a rolled-up newspaper or a paper towel.
- Continue to push in the pilot light knob for approximately one minute and then slowly release it.
- If the pilot flame goes out, wait five minutes to allow the accumulated gas to dissipate and repeat the process.
- When the pilot light remains on, turn the thermostat control knob to the desired temperature.
- If the equipment is equipped with a power switch, you have to turn it to the ON position.

RANGES

Overview

FIGURE 5.1

Source: Vulcan.

There are many different styles of ranges, all of which have a specific job to do. First, they can be fueled by either gas or electricity. The type of cookery that needs to be done determines which style of range to choose. There are four types of range surfaces (see Figure 5.1).

- **Solid surface**—Called hot tops or flat tops, these offer a flat solid surface on the range, which allows for several pots and pans of different shapes and sizes to be in use at one time. While the surface has hotter spots and cooler spots, it does not have precise temperature control for each individual pot or pan. They are used primarily for batch cooking and stockpots.
- **French plate**—An individual cooking surface that can accommodate one pot or pan and whose temperature is individually controlled. A round cast iron plate covers the heating element. It is used for smaller stockpots and short-order, small-batch cooking.
- **Open burner** (also called a spider)—Gas fired only, this has a metal grate that holds the pot or pan over the open flame. It is also individually controlled and is used for small stockpots and small-batch cooking, as well as for short orders and sautéing.
- **Cal rod**—Electric only, the pot or pan is placed directly on the cal rod unit. It is individually controlled and used for short-orders and small-batch cooking.

 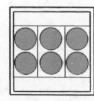 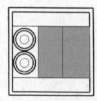 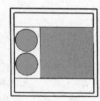 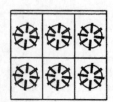 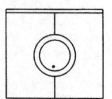

FIGURE 5.2 Range top surfaces. Left to right: flat top, French plate, 1/3 cal rod 2/3 flat top, 1/3 French plate 2/3 flat top, open burner, gas flat top.

Source: Vulcan.

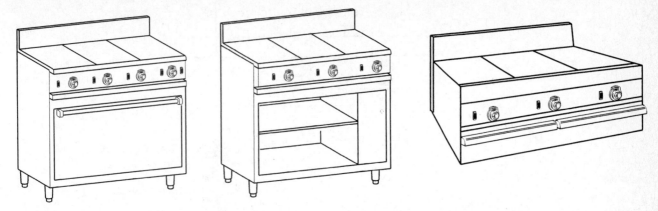

FIGURE 5.3 Left to right: range top with oven underneath, range top with cabinet underneath, countertop range.
Source: Vulcan.

A range can contain one of these surfaces exclusively or a combination of them. Almost all manufacturers make their range tops in 12-inch increments. Thus, on a 36-inch range you could have three combinations, a 48-inch range four combinations, and a 60-inch range five combinations. A range could be all flat top or two-thirds flattop and one-third open burner or any other combination you desire. The possibilities are practically endless.

One thing that is normally not done because of cost constraints is to combine gas and electric. Thus your range should be either all gas or all electric.

Use common sense when choosing which range in the kitchen you use to perform a specific task. It would not make sense to place a large stockpot filled with water and expect it to come to a boil quickly on a French plate or open burner. Conversely, it would not make sense to cook a temperature-sensitive item on a flat top with other items all cooking at a higher or lower temperature.

While most ranges come with an oven underneath them, they can also be purchased alone and placed on a stand with shelving underneath. They can also be purchased as a counter model and placed on a cooking line sitting on a cabinet. (Figure 5.3 shows these three options.)

Parts

- Range top burner control knobs—Turns the range on and off and determines the temperature.
- Oven control knob—If applicable, turns the oven on and off, as well as controls the oven temperature (covered in detail in the oven section).

Operation

WARNING: The range and its parts are hot. Use care when operating and cleaning the range. Always use heavy-duty pot holders when removing pots or pans.

ALL RANGES   Be sure to use pots and pans that have a flat bottom and straight sides. This puts the pot or pan in direct contact with the cooking surface and greatly speeds up the cooking process. As pots and pans get older, the bottoms tend to bow out, particularly those used on electric ranges.

On hot top or flat top ranges, do not use the cooking surface as a griddle. It is not built for this purpose and will result in a poorly cooked product. It also creates a fire hazard because grease can work its way down to the heating elements or burners.

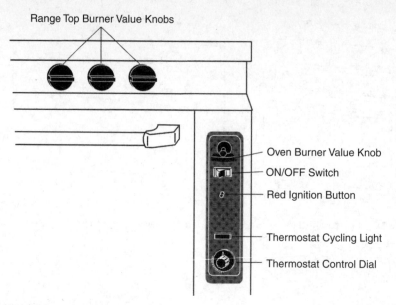

Range Top Burner Value Knobs

Oven Burner Value Knob

ON/OFF Switch

Red Ignition Button

Thermostat Cycling Light

Thermostat Control Dial

FIGURE 5.4 Range top control knobs with an oven control panel on the right.
Source: Vulcan.

GAS RANGES To turn on a range top equipped with gas, turn the burner valve knob counterclockwise to the HIGH position until the burner ignites. After ignition, adjust the flame by turning it clockwise to the desired temperature. On most ranges, counterclockwise opens the burner, increases the gas flow, increases the flame, and increases the temperature. Clockwise reduces the gas flow, lowers the flame, lowers the temperature, and closes the valve.

On ranges equipped with open burners, each burner is controlled by its own separate burner valve knob. Normally the left-hand control knob is used for the rear burner, and the right-hand control knob is used for the front burner.

On center-fired hot top or flat top ranges, all burners should be turned on HIGH to heat the top quickly. Once the operating temperature is reached, some of the rings should be turned down or off. On hot tops, the heat is distributed over the entire surface; therefore, fewer burners need to be used. Because the heat is concentrated in the center of the range, this area should be used to bring the product to a boil, at which time it can then be moved over to maintain a rolling boil or to the side of the flat top for a simmer.

ELECTRIC RANGES When using electric range tops, bring the temperature of the surface unit to the correct temperature before cooking the product. In other words, do not put the product on a cold range; turn the unit on and wait for it to come to the proper temperature. On most hot top or flat top ranges, each hot top section can be controlled independently.

There are two types of hot top ranges. One has HIGH, MEDIUM, or LOW settings and is used primarily for batch cooking or stockpots. The other is equipped with a thermostat, which allows for a variety of temperature settings for sautéing, braising, and pan frying. On ranges equipped with French plates or cal rods, each burner is independently operated. Some products require quick changes from hot to low heat levels. Since electric cooking is slow to respond to variations in temperature, it is recommended that different surface sections be set at different temperatures. In this way, pots or pans can be shifted from one section to another to change the cooking speed.

Cleaning

Before cleaning any range or oven, disconnect the power source. Electric ranges are normally direct-wired, which means that the power will have to be shut off at the electric control panel. Flip the circuit breaker switch to the OFF position and tag the switch as to the fact that the equipment is being worked on.

On a daily basis, or as necessary during the shift, flat top or hot top ranges (gas or electric) should have the grease drain and trough wiped down and the grease pan emptied. While the cooking surface is still warm (not hot), wipe it down with a cloth to remove spills, grease, and food particles. Product that is allowed to burn into the surface will form a crust and will interfere with the efficiency of the range. Do not use steel wool to clean the range top. If the spill is difficult to remove, soak it with hot soapy water. After cleaning, the surface of the cast iron flat top should be re-seasoned. Pour a small amount of cooking oil (1 ounce per square foot/28 grams per 0.09 square meters) on the surface. Wipe off any excess oil and turn the burners or heating elements on low for two hours. This will resist cracking of the cast iron and will ensure longer life of the heating surface.

On gas ranges equipped with open top burners, remove the grates and clean under and around the burners. Remove the drip pan located under the burners, empty it, and clean it in the pot and pan sink with a nonabrasive detergent.

The surface of the range—whether it is painted enamel, stainless steel, or brushed aluminum—should be cleaned with a mild nonabrasive detergent mixed with water, according to the manufacturer's directions. After cleaning, it should be wiped down with a dry soft cloth. Do not use scouring powder, steel wool, or metal sponges to clean the exterior of the range. If the surface is stainless steel, a polish can be applied and the excess wiped off with a soft dry cloth. Occasionally, stainless steel surfaces will get a darkened or straw-colored area around the range surface or the oven. This is called heat tint and is brought about by excessive heat (500°F [260°C] or more) over a period of time causing an oxidation of the stainless steel. This can be removed by applying a commercial heat tint remover.

Maintenance

Gas ranges require that the burner ports be kept clean. Check these weekly. To clean the burner ports, remove them and boil in a strong solution of lye water for 15–20 minutes. Then brush them with a wire brush.

The burners should have a blue flame. Excess yellow in the flame indicates an excessive mixture of air to gas. Contact your local gas service company and have a representative adjust the flame.

Electric ranges require no maintenance.

INDUCTION COOKTOP

Overview

Induction cooking is fast catching on in commercial equipment. It is a relatively new concept, differing drastically from the traditional gas burner or electric element method of cooking. Rather than heating a pan from a heat source, it heats the pan by transferring magnetic waves.

Induction systems use basically two parts: an inductor, which is the magnetic source, and the receiver, which is the pan.

FIGURE 5.5

Source: Vulcan.

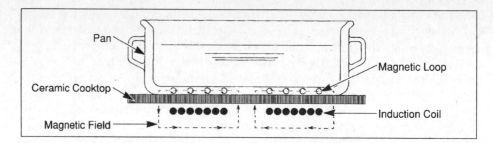

FIGURE 5.6 Inductor transferring a magnetic field to the receiver (utensil or pan).

Electrical current goes into the induction coil and creates a magnetic field. When a pan is placed on the ceramic cooktop, it completes the field and causes the molecules in the pan to move very quickly. The resulting friction between the molecules causes the pan to become hot. The interesting thing is that the only heat on the cooking surface is the heat conducted from the pan. Thus a kitchen using induction cooktops is much cooler than a kitchen using the conventional gas or electric cooktops. When the pan is removed from the cooktop, the molecules quit agitating and the cooking process stops. Figure 5.6 demonstrates how an induction cooktop works.

For the system to work, the pan needs to be magnetic. Therefore, a pan made of cast iron, enameled iron, or stainless steel with an inner layer of iron is best. Other pans are acceptable if a magnet will adhere to the side of the pan. Aluminum, copper, earthenware, or heat-resistant glass pans will not work. Choose a pan that has a flat bottom and is 5–10 $\frac{1}{2}$ inches (127–266.7 millimeter) in diameter. Pans with a bowed bottom, pans with feet or a rim on the bottom, or Chinese woks will not work.

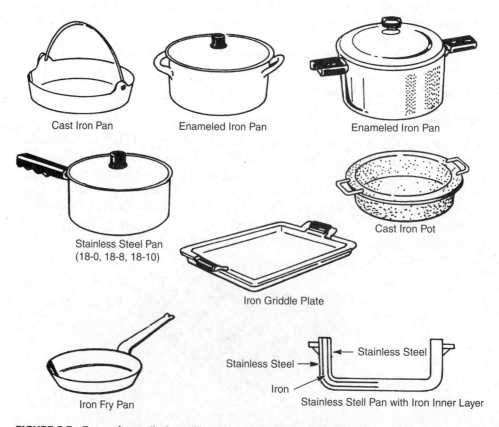

FIGURE 5.7 Types of utensils that will work on an induction cooktop.

Some cautions in working with induction cooktops are:

- The ceramic top could be hot after use by conduction from the pan.
- The ceramic top is breakable. Do not drop heavy objects on it.
- Do not place the cooktop near a radio, television, or remote-controlled equipment.
- Do not place metal items such as foil, metal cans, spatulas, or flatware on the cooking surface.
- Keep magnetic items (such as computer discs, magnetic tapes, cassettes, credit cards, magnetic tickets, or hotel passkeys) away from the cooktop.

Parts

- Control knob—Turns the cooktop on to the desired temperature and also turns the unit off (see Figure 5.8).
- Indicator light—Indicates the cooktop status. If the light is steady, the unit is cooking. If the light is blinking, the unit is in standby mode.

Operation

Place the pan with product to be cooked on the ceramic cooktop surface. Turn the unit on by rotating the control knob clockwise to the desired cooking level. The cooling fan will come on and the indicator light will illuminate steadily. If the indicator light flashes, this means that the unit is in standby mode and will shut off after three minutes in this mode. If this happens, the unit must be reset by turning the control knob to the OFF position and then on to the desired temperature. The primary cause for the cooktop going to the standby mode is that the unit does not detect a pan on the cooking surface. Make sure that the pan being used is made out of the recommended material.

When a high temperature is being used, 380°F (193°C) or higher, the indicator light will flash intermittently and then return to a continuous light. This indicates that the unit is cycling between ON and STANDBY to maintain the proper operating temperature. When cooking is completed, turn the control knob to the OFF position. The fans will continue to run until the unit is completely cooled.

Cleaning

Disconnect the electrical power before cleaning. Clean the ceramic cooktop surface with a cloth that has been moistened in a solution of detergent and warm water. Rinse and dry. For stubborn stains, you may use a soft paste cleanser. Do not use any abrasive cleaners, stainless steel pads, or metal sponges because they could damage the ceramic surface. The front and sides of the cooktop can be wiped down with a clean cloth and a stainless steel cleaner and polish.

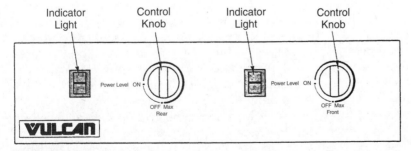

FIGURE 5.8 Control panel for an induction cooktop.

Source: Vulcan.

Maintenance

The air filter(s) should be cleaned monthly. They are located on the bottom of the cooktop and will simply snap out. Wash them in a sink with a solution of soap and hot water, rinse thoroughly, dry completely, and replace. Do not attempt to use the induction cooktop without the air filter(s).

GRIDDLE

Overview

Griddles are used for griddling short-order items. They are popular for preparing breakfast items such as pancakes, French toast, bacon, sausage, hash browned potatoes, eggs, and omelets. They can also be used for sandwich items such as grilled cheese, Reuben's, and hamburgers as well as for some entrée items. Griddles are heated by either gas or electric elements.

Of the several different styles of griddle plate surfaces, all affect the cooking time and temperature. The most common surface is that of cast iron. This is the original griddle plate surface and is so sturdy that it hardly ever wears out; hence its popularity. It is being replaced on today's market by surfaces of polished steel and chrome plate. The polished steel and chrome plate surfaces are less porous than that of the cast iron; and consequently, food sticks less and they are easier to clean. They also tend to have an improved transfer of heat to the product. Regardless of the type of surface, the thicker the griddle, the more even the cooking temperature. A 1-inch thick griddle produces a more even heat than a $\frac{3}{4}$-inch griddle.

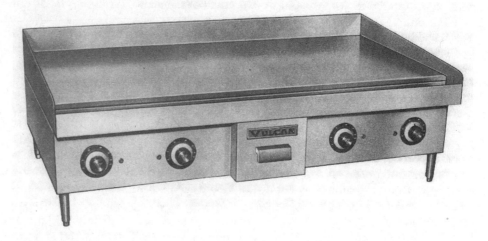

FIGURE 5.9

Source: Vulcan.

Parts

- Griddle plate—The surface on which the product is cooked. Can be constructed of chrome, stainless steel, or cast iron (see Figure 5.10).
- Side splash or rear splash—A protective metal wall to prevent grease and food particles from falling onto the worktable or counter surface.
- Grease trough—A channel on the front or rear of the griddle to collect grease and food particles and direct them into the grease drawer.
- Grease drawer—A pan located under the griddle surface to collect excess grease and food particles from the grease trough.
- Thermostat dial—Turns the griddle on and off and determines the temperature setting of the griddle surface.
- Chassis—The exterior surface or faceplate of the griddle.

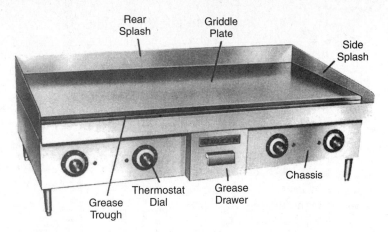

FIGURE 5.10   Parts of a griddle.

Source: Vulcan.

Operation

SEASONING THE GRIDDLE   While the cooking area of the griddle appears to be a smooth surface, in reality it is covered with tiny microscopic pores. Food that is being cooked tends to get caught in these pores and stick. Therefore, prior to using the griddle, it is necessary to season it by filling up these pores with oil. This gives the metal surface a slick hard finish from which the food will release easily.

To season the griddle, turn it on to a moderate 300–350°F (150–164°C) setting. Cover the entire griddle surface with a thin coat of vegetable or other cooking oil, about 1 ounce of oil per square foot of surface. Wait for two minutes and use a clean cloth to wipe off any excess oil. The griddle is now ready for use.

OPERATING THE GRIDDLE   Preheat the griddle by turning the thermostat dial to the desired cooking temperature. For most griddles, the preheat time is 15–20 minutes. On electric models, a red light comes on when the thermostat dial is turned on. When the designated temperature is reached, the red light goes out. Thereafter, the light will be on or off while the heating element is on or off. On most griddles, each thermostat controls a 12-inch wide section, thus you can have several different temperatures on the griddle surface (see Figure 5.11).

Always keep the griddle surface clean while cooking. After each cooking load, scrape the griddle surface with a spatula to remove excess oil, carbon, and food particles. On chrome surfaces, to reduce carbonized grease buildup, flush the surface with water and scrape with the customized spatula that comes with the griddle. Carbonized grease buildup on the griddle surface hinders the transfer of heat from the surface to the food, resulting in spotty browning. The grease buildup also clings to the food, giving it an unsatisfactory taste and appearance.

When cooking on the griddle, avoid banging the spatula on the griddle surface to loosen food. While the surface appears to be quite hard, in reality it is soft and can be nicked, dented, or gouged easily. This will result in foods sticking and not being evenly browned. Also avoid pushing or pressing against the side and back splashes as they can easily be pushed away from the griddle surface, allowing grease to get caught between them.

Cleaning

In addition to scraping the griddle after each use and occasionally flushing a chrome surface with water to reduce the carbonized grease, it is necessary to thoroughly clean the griddle after each shift.

- Use a degreaser with water on chrome and a pumice stone on steel and cast iron. Do not use water on cast iron. Do not use steel wool on any griddle surface.

Suggested Cooking Guide

FOOD	THERMOSTAT SETTING °F	TIME IN MIN.
Sandwich Items		
Hamburgers	350	3-4
Cheeseburgers	350	3-4
Cheese Sandwiches	375	3-4
Ham Salad Sandwiches	375	3-4
Meats		
Frankfurters	325	2-3
Minute Steak-medium	400	3-4
Club Steaks - thick, medium	400	3-5
Ham Steaks	375	3-4
Beef Tenderloin	400	3-4
Boiled Ham	375	2
Corned Beef Patties	350	2-3
Bacon	350	2-3
Canadian Bacon	350	2-3
Sausage Links	350	3
Sausage Patties	350	3
Eggs		
Scrambled	300	1-2
Hard Fried	300	3
Soft Fried	300	2
Sunny Side Up	300	2
Other		
French Toast	350	2-3
Pancakes	375	2
American Fries	375	3-4
Potato Patties	375	3-4

FIGURE 5.11   Cooking time and temperature for grilled foods.

- Clean the surface while it is still warm. Always rub the griddle surface in the same direction as the grain of the metal.
- After cleaning, make sure that the surface is completely clean and devoid of any degreaser or pumice stone particles. Customers are picky about finding little black spots on their over-easy eggs in the morning.
- Thoroughly wipe out and clean the grease trough.
- Remove the grease drawer, empty it in the grease barrel, wash it out in the pot and pan sink, and put it back.
- Clean the back splash and side splashes with a damp cloth. If excess food is stuck on the splashes or if discoloring occurs, a nonabrasive cleaner can be used.
- Clean the stainless steel front exterior of the griddle with a damp cloth and polish it with a soft dry cloth. If desired, a stainless steel cleaner and polish can be used.
- After cleaning, the griddle surface must be re-seasoned to avoid having food stuck to it.

Maintenance

There is no maintenance to be performed on the griddle.

FRYER

Overview

Deep fat fryers are used in many commercial kitchens and come in gas or electric as well as stationary or table models. While they are very useful, the high temperature at which they function makes them very dangerous to operate as well as to clean. Fryers normally operate at 350°F (176°C), but there are exceptions. Consult your recipe or product directions for the proper temperature.

One of the major expenses of operating a fryer is the cost of shortening or oil. As a matter of fact, the Keating Company estimates that the cost of oil over the lifetime of the fryer is greater than the cost of the system itself. Prudent operators, therefore, want to ensure that the life of the shortening is as extensive as possible while still delivering an excellent product. Food cooked at too low a temperature in old oil will deliver a soggy brown product, while food cooked at the proper temperature in satisfactory oil will product a crisp, crunchy, golden brown product. It's a fact of life that shortening breaks down as it is used, but handled properly it can last much longer than if handled improperly. To ensure the longevity of oil or shortening, follow these steps:

FIGURE 5.12
Source: Garland.

- Filter the oil daily.
- Boil the system out weekly.
- Oxygen breaks down oil. The hotter the oil, the greater the breakdown. Always cook at the proper temperature.
- For the same reason, keep the fryer at a low temperature during slack periods. Not only will it prolong the life of the shortening, it will also lower utility costs.
- Keep the kettle covered when not in use.
- Carefully remove crumbs and food particles that fall off the food by using a strainer. Those not removed will eventually carbonize and cause shortening breakdown.
- Salt and seasonings containing sodium and sodium byproducts break down oil. Potatoes treated with sodium sulfite to retain whiteness should be washed and completely dried prior to frying.

Parts

- Power ON switch—Turns the unit on and shuts if off. *Note:* Some manufacturers do not have a power switch. Setting the thermostat to the desired temperature simultaneously turns the unit's power on.
- Thermostat—Controls the cooking temperature.
- Drain valve—The valve that allows the oil to drain from the kettle when emptying and/or cleaning the fryer. This should always be closed when filling the kettle with shortening or oil.
- Kettle—The vessel that holds the shortening where the product is fried.
- Melt cycle—Used to melt solid shortening (not available on all models).

Operation

FILLING THE FRYER   Fryers can operate with either liquid or solid shortening. While scientists and chefs argue the merits of each, when it comes to safety in the process of filling the fryer, liquid is preferred.

CAUTION: Before filling the fryer with either liquid or solid shortening, make sure that the drain valve is completely closed. This, like most cautions, seems redundant. But consider that, if the drain is open, the shortening when poured into the fryer will flow right out of the fryer onto the floor and spread out over the kitchen, leaving a slippery, oily mess that will take hours to clean up. (This will happen only once in your career.)

When filling the fryer with liquid shortening (after ascertaining that the drain valve is closed) simply pour the liquid shortening into the tank up to the Oil

Level or the Fill to line. Do not go over this line because oil expands when it is heated and is also displaced when product is placed in the fryer. Going over the line when filling could result in the oil boiling over and causing serious injury. When the kettle is properly filled, turn the unit on and set the temperature thermostat. Many models have a HEAT or HEATING light that goes on while the unit is heating up. When it reaches its proper temperature, a READY or COOK light goes on. The fryer is now ready for use.

When using solid shortening, again make sure the drain valve is closed and cut the shortening into small cubes. Pack the shortening in the tank above, under, and around the tubes if using a gas fryer or around the elements if using electric. Do not leave any air gaps. Be careful not to bend or break the temperature probe in this process, because the fryer will not operate properly if this happens. Never melt a solid block of shortening on top of the burner tubes; this could result in a fire (see Figure 5.13).

If the unit is equipped with an automatic melting cycle, turn it on. On most fryers, for the melt cycle to work, the fryer must also be turned to the ON position. With the automatic melt cycle, the fryer will intermittently turn on and off until the shortening is melted and its temperature is 150°F (65°C). At this point, the burners or elements will remain on until the shortening reaches the temperature setting on the thermostat and the READY or COOK (if applicable) light goes on. At this point, make certain that the oil is at the FILL TO or OIL LEVEL line. The unit is now ready for use.

If the unit is not equipped with an automatic melting cycle, cut and pack the solid shortening as just described. Turn the unit on for 4 seconds and off for 30 seconds. If at any time you notice smoke, this indicates that the shortening is scorching. Reduce the amount of time that the unit is in the ON position. Repeat the cycle until most of the solid shortening has turned into a liquid and the temperature has reached 150°F (65°C). Set the thermostat to the desired temperature and leave the fryer in the ON position. When it reaches the desired temperature, it is ready for use.

FRYER OPERATION

- Turn the unit on by turning the power switch to the ON or FRY position.
- Set the thermostat to the desired temperature, normally 350°F (176°C). When the unit has indicated that it has heated up to the proper cooking temperature, it is ready for use.
- Place the product to be cooked into the basket. Do not overfill the basket as the product will not cook evenly, and it could also be a danger to the operator.
- Carefully lower the basket into the kettle. Avoid splashing the hot oil. If the product has excessive ice crystals, if it is damp, or if the temperature of the oil is too high, spattering occurs. *Note:* Water and hot oil do not mix. Always stand back and to the side when lowering the basket.

When the product is completely cooked:

- Lift the basket out of the oil and place it on the basket hanger.
- Do not bang the basket on the hanger or the kettle.

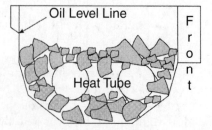

FIGURE 5.13 Air gaps in solid shortening placed in a fryer tank. Solid shortening should be packed tightly to avoid air gaps.

- Allow the basket to drain completely.
- Do not lift the basket out of the kettle and go directly to the holding pan without draining the basket first.

On units equipped with basket lifts, proceed as just explained, but:

- Place the basket on the upper bar of the lift rod.
- Set the timer to the proper cooking time and push the START button. The basket will automatically lower itself into the kettle.
- When the time has elapsed and the cooking is complete, the basket will rise automatically and an alarm will sound.

Cleaning

DAILY CLEANING AND FILTERING   To maintain a quality-looking fryer and to assure that it works at its peak, clean the exterior daily. Wipe off any oil spills immediately with a clean soft cloth while the oil is still warm and before it hardens. To remove stains, use a mild detergent or a nonabrasive scouring powder. Be extremely careful not to get any water in the frying tank.

The oil in the fryer should be filtered daily. In operations that fry a high volume of breaded products, it may be necessary to filter several times during the day. Frequent filtering prolongs the life of the shortening, since particles that fall off in the frying process continue to fry in the oil, causing it to break down.

When carrying out the filtering process, remember that the temperature of the oil exceeds 300°F (150°C), and great care should be exercised to avoid injury and burns. It is strongly recommended that oil-proof insulated gloves, an oil- and heat-resistant apron, and safety goggles be worn during the filtering procedure.

DAILY MANUAL FILTERING   Manually filtering the oil in the fryer is one of the most dangerous tasks performed in the kitchen, and extreme care and sound judgment should be exercised at all times. The materials needed are:

- A heavy-duty, covered container.
- A cone-shaped filter holder.
- Cone-shaped paper filters.
- A drain extension.
- Oil-proof insulated gloves.
- Safety goggles.
- Heat resistant apron.

Make sure that the stockpot you are using has a capacity that is greater than the capacity of the fryer tank. Use only a heavy-duty metal stockpot. Do not use a plastic "pickle bucket" or any other plastic bucket because the hot oil will melt the plastic.

To filter the shortening:

1. Make sure that the fryer is turned off but the oil is still hot enough to flow (300°C). This is important particularly if you are using a solid shortening.
2. Screw the drain extension onto the drain line of the fryer. (On some models, this step is not necessary.)
3. Place the paper filter into the filter holder.
4. Place the filter holder on the stockpot.
5. Place the container under the drain so that, when it is opened, the oil will drain through the paper filter and into the container.
6. Open the drain.
7. Using the brush, knock the crumbs into the oil as it drains from the fryer tank.
8. When the oil has completely drained, wipe down the fryer tank with a soft cloth towel.
9. Remove, empty, and clean the crumb strainer and replace.
10. Close the drain.

11. Remove the drain extension.
12. Double check to make sure the drain is closed. Carefully lift the container and pour the oil back into the fryer tank. For large fryers, two people should perform this task.
13. Add new shortening as necessary to bring the level back up to the FILL line.
14. Remove the filter paper holder from the container and discard the paper filter.

For smaller electric table model fryers, the procedure is somewhat simplified, although still dangerous:

1. Lift the electric elements out of the fryer tank and lock them into place. At this point, the elements will be up in the air over the tank.
2. Lift the tank carefully by its handles and pour the oil into the paper filter in the filter holder on the stockpot.
3. Wipe down the fryer tank using a clean soft cloth and return it to the fryer.
4. Release the element catch and lower the electric elements into the fryer tank.
5. Discard the filter paper and pour the oil back into the fryer tank.

DAILY POWER FILTERING   Two types of filtering systems are available: built-in and portable. Since the portable system is a little more detailed than the built-in system, the portable system will be covered here.

1. Heat oil in the fryer to 300°F.
2. With a pair of tongs, remove the screen over the tubes or heating elements.
3. Turn the fryer to the OFF position.
4. In the filter tub, insert the filter screen, insert filter paper on top of the filter screen, and add cleaning powder on top of the filter paper.
5. Insert the strainer basket into the filter tub.
6. Place the filter tub under the fryer drain, open the drain valve, and allow the hot oil to drain into the filter tub.
7. Turn the pump to the ON position, and using the hose, flush down the sides of the oil cavity in the fryer. Make sure that all particles are flushed out.
8. Clean the fryer kettle with a nonabrasive scrub pad and cleanser. Rinse the fryer kettle down with hot oil from the filter.
9. Pump the filtered oil back into the fryer kettle.

WEEKLY BOIL-OUT   As already discussed, put on the proper safety attire, then drain and filter the oil in the fryer, prior to performing the boil-out procedure.

1. Move the filtered shortening to a secure area to prevent accidental spillage.
2. Making sure that the drain is closed; fill the kettle to the FILL line with water.

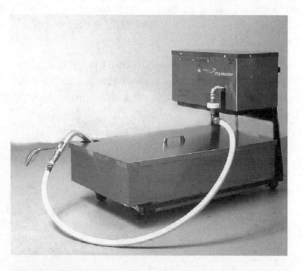

FIGURE 5.14   Portable power filtering equipment.
Source: Garland.

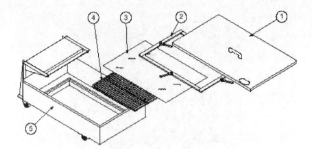

FIGURE 5.15   The parts of a filter system. 1) Filter pan cover, 2) Filter screen, 3) Filter paper, 4) Crumb tray, 5) Filter pan.
Source: Garland.

3. Set the thermostat and turn the fryer on. When the water reaches a gentle boil, turn the fryer off. Do not leave the fryer during this operation since it could boil over.
4. Add an approved cleansing agent to the water and let soak for a half hour. *Note:* Follow the directions on the cleaning agent package, as some recommend adding the product prior to boiling and some direct a different length of time for the soaking procedure.
5. Using a long-handled brush, scrub down the sides of the kettle as well as the heating tubes. Be extremely careful because the hot water can cause a severe burn on your skin.
6. Drain the water and the cleaning agent into a suitable container and discard.
7. If any crumbs or carbonized oil are still adhering to the sides or heating tubes, scrub these off with a brush. In the case of stubborn sediment, a nonabrasive scouring pad may be used.
8. Thoroughly rinse the unit with clean water to remove all of the cleansing agent. Wipe down the inside of the kettle, making sure that all the water has been removed. Again, water and hot oil do not mix.
9. Close the drain and fill the kettle with either the filtered shortening or with new oil.

Maintenance

Weekly—Drain, clean, and boil out the fryer (see above).

Monthly—Verify thermostat settings.

Annually—Clean the burner orifices (gas only), calibrate the thermostat—these duties to be performed by qualified service personnel only.

PROOFING CABINET/HOT HOLDING CABINET

Overview

The operating and cleaning characteristics for proofing cabinets and for hot food holding cabinets are virtually identical (with a few exceptions) and are consequently combined here. As a matter of fact, some companies manufacture models that will handle both functions, and many small operations use the same cabinet for both tasks.

PROOFING CABINETS   One of the basic steps in the production of yeast products is the **proofing process**. It is a critical step, in that an under-proofed product has a dense texture and a lower yield. On the other hand, a product that is over-proofed has a coarse texture and loses some of its flavor potential. The proper proofing procedure has three components: temperature, humidity, and time. To control temperature and humidity, a proofing cabinet, also called a proof box, is used. Set

FIGURE 5.16
Source: Cres Cor.

the temperature to 95°F (36°C) and 85 percent humidity. Leave the product in the proof box until it has doubled in volume.

HOT HOLDING CABINETS   Holding cabinets are used to keep hot product at a safe holding temperature from the time it has finished the preparation stage until it is served. They are not designed to reheat food. Food that is placed in holding cabinets can be either in bulk (steam table pans) or plated. Used primarily for banquet, buffet, or cafeteria service, the holding cabinet is a necessary piece of equipment to keep the product hot and out of the danger zone. It is, however, not kind to product quality. To reduce deterioration, food should be kept in the holding cabinet for the shortest period of time possible. The product should also be kept at a minimum temperature of 140°F (60°C).

Parts

- Power switch—Turns the unit on or off (see Figure 5.17).
- Indicator light—Indicates that the cabinet power is on. On some models there are separate lights for the power switch, proofing, and holding.
- Thermostat—Sets both the cabinet air temperature and humidity. On some models, the cabinet air temperature and the humidity have separate thermostats.
- Heating element—Heats the cabinet as well as the water to create humidity.
- Water pan—Holds the water to create the humidity inside the cabinet (see Figure 5.18).

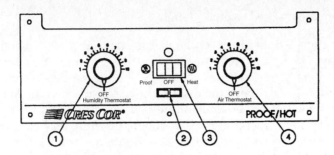

Control Panel Parts Identification

1. Thermostat-Humidity   3. Switch
2. Indicator Lights   4. Thermostat-Air

The thermometer shows the temperature inside cabinet.

FIGURE 5.17 Control panel of a holding cabinet/proofing cabinet.

Source: Cres Cor.

Operation

To properly utilize the proofing/holding cabinet, follow these steps:

1. Turn the power switch to ON. On most models, a light comes on, indicating that the unit is in the operating mode.
2. Turn the thermostat to high or 10, depending on the model.
3. Let the cabinet preheat for 30 minutes.

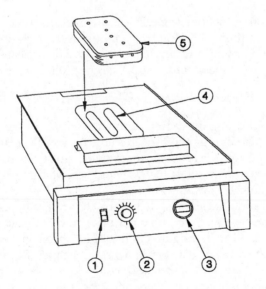

Parts Identification

1. Power Switch
2. Thermostat
3. Temperature Display
4. Heater
5. Water Pan with cover

FIGURE 5.18 The lower section of a holding cabinet/proofing cabinet that contains the control panel and water pan.

Source: Cres Cor.

If the cabinet is being used to proof dough:

- Follow steps 1–3 and then set the thermostat to 95°F (35°C) and 85 percent humidity. Some models have one control for temperature and humidity, while others have separate controls. Still other models have a numbered thermostat (1–10). Check the manufacturer's instructions as to which number gives you the proper temperature and humidity.
- Put fresh dough, or if using frozen dough, put fully thawed dough into the cabinet. *Note:* Do not place frozen dough into the cabinet. If frozen or even cold-thawed dough is placed into the cabinet, the temperature will drop significantly.
- Close the door.
- Check the water level in the water pan from time to time. If additional water is needed, fill with hot water.

If the cabinet is being used to hold product:

- Follow steps 1–3 and place the hot product into the cabinet.
- Set the thermostat to the desired temperature. Remember that to keep food out of the danger zone, the temperature must be a minimum of 140°F (60°C). Also note that the higher the temperature, the quicker the food will dry out and deteriorate. Experimentation is necessary to ensure both the safety of the customer and the quality level of the food.
- Close the door.

When you are through using the proofing cabinet, turn the thermostat and the power switch to the OFF position.

Cleaning

DOOR   Many proofing/hot holding cabinets are manufactured with glass or plastic see-through door. If this is the case, clean the glass or plastic either with a mild detergent and water or with a weak alcohol-type window cleaner.

If the door is solid metal (aluminum), clean it following the same directions as for the cabinet.

CABINET   Prior to cleaning the cabinet, allow it to cool and then unplug the cord set from the wall. Also unplug the cord from the back of the cabinet, by turning it counterclockwise to unlock it. Next, remove the hot unit from the cabinet by sliding it out. *Note:* Some models have several screws that need to be removed prior to removing the hot unit.

While most proofing cabinets are constructed of aluminum, check to make sure that this is the case with your cabinet prior to cleaning it. The interior and exterior can be cleaned with a damp cloth that has been soaked in a solution of mild detergent and water, or use a mild abrasive cleaner. Rinse the cabinet with hot water and wipe it dry with a soft clean cloth. For heavy stains, grease or oil, a chemical oven cleaner (specifically formulated for aluminum) can be used. Follow the manufacturer's directions for use. When using detergent, abrasives, or oven cleaners, always make a spot test in a small hidden area to make sure that the product will not damage the cabinet surface. Never mix cleaners. If desired, the proofing cabinet can also be steam cleaned.

Maintenance

Empty and clean the water pan once a week. It may be necessary to use a solution to de-scale or de-lime the pan, depending on the water conditions in the area.

COFFEE BREWING EQUIPMENT

Overview

One of the most important products coming out of the kitchen is coffee. Many restaurants are judged by the quality of their coffee. Coffee can be brewed in large batches in an urn or in small batches by the pot. Since coffee deteriorates rather quickly after it is brewed, it is critical that the correct equipment be chosen to serve a quality product.

Urns are best when a large amount of coffee needs to be produced in a short period of time. Operations such as large institutions or banquet kitchens would probably find that an urn best suits their needs. For most operations, the urns have a 3-gallon capacity, although they can be larger, going up to 125 gallons. They can be fully automated or manually operated. In a manual operation, the person brewing the coffee physically pours the hot water over the coffee grounds. This is a highly dangerous procedure, not to mention that the quality of the coffee is dependent on the person pouring the correct amount of boiling water over the grounds. For these reasons, it is recommended that the automated urn be used.

Small restaurants or other operations where the demand is not as high would be best served by using decanter brewing. In this system, coffee is brewed in individual pots normally containing 10 serving cups. Equipment that utilizes instant coffee powder, freeze-dried, or liquid coffee concentrate is also available, although the quality of these products is questionable. A system very similar to decanter brewing is the airpot system. As its operation is identical to the decanter system, they are covered together in this chapter.

Parts

URN BREWING

- Dial thermometer—Indicates when the water is at the proper brewing temperature.
- Funnel—Holds the coffee filter.
- Funnel cover—Covers the funnel and has an opening on the top for hot water from the water spout to enter the funnel and spray water over the coffee grounds.
- Water swing spout—A water spout that can be swung from the left urn to the right urn allowing hot water to be sprayed over the coffee grounds in the funnel.

FIGURE 5.19 Twin 3-gallon coffee urn with a hot water tank in the center.

Source: Bunn-O-Matic.

- ON/OFF switch—Allows the brewing mechanism to be activated and turns on the heat to the reservoir.
- Start switch—Activates the brewing mechanism.
- Reservoir—The container that holds the brewed coffee.
- Sight gauge—A clear glass tube that indicates the level of coffee in the reservoir.
- Faucet—A device that allows the coffee or hot water to be drained from the reservoir.

DECANTER AND AIRPOT BREWING

- ON/OFF switch—Allows the brewing mechanism to be activated and turns on the heat to the brew station warmer.
- Start switch—Activates a brew cycle.
- Funnel—Holds the coffee filter.
- Funnel rails—Holds the funnel.
- Sprayhead—Sprays the water over the coffee grounds in the filter in the funnel.

Operation

URN BREWING Prior to brewing coffee, ascertain that the water is at the correct temperature of 200°F (93°C). The temperature is indicated on the thermometer. To brew a perfect cup of coffee:

- Insert a paper filter into the funnel.
- Place the desired amount of coffee needed in the paper filter. In most cases, the coffee is pre-portioned in a package by the coffee company. When bulk coffee

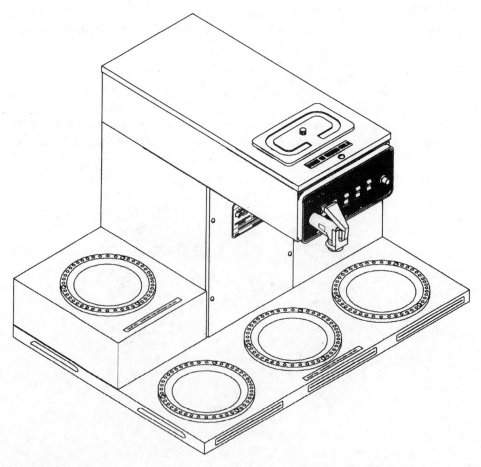

FIGURE 5.20 Decanter brewing station with hot water valve and auxiliary warmers.
Source: Bunn-O-Matic.

is used, portion the correct amount according to the restaurant's standards. Spread the grounds evenly in the filter to assure uniform extraction.

- Place the funnel onto the funnel support.
- Place the funnel cover over the funnel.
- Place the water swing spout over the hole in the center of the funnel cover.
- Turn the ON/OFF switch to the ON position.
- Push the START switch once. Do not move the water swing spout until the brewing cycle has been completed.
- When the brewing cycle has been completed, move the water swing spout to the center of the machine. Remove the funnel cover and remove the funnel. Do not leave the grounds in the funnel after the brewing has been completed—this results in a bitter-tasting cup of coffee.
- Empty the funnel by turning it upside down over a waste container to dispose of the paper filter and grounds.
- Hold the coffee at 185°F (85°C). Holding it at a higher temperature causes it to break down and become bitter.

During the brewing cycle, small amounts of hot water may be drawn from the center (water) urn. However, if a large amount (over 1 gallon) of water is needed, wait until the brewing cycle has been completed. Filters should be stored in a filter holder to prevent the sides from collapsing. Collapsed filter sides fall over in the funnel, resulting in coffee grounds flowing over into the urn and ultimately into the customer's cup of coffee.

DECANTER AND AIRPOT BREWING

- Insert a paper filter into the funnel.
- Place the desired amount of coffee needed in the paper filter. In most cases, the coffee is pre-portioned in a package by the coffee company and sometimes it is even in its own filter. When bulk coffee is used, portion the correct amount according to the restaurant's standards.
- Slide the funnel into the funnel rails.
- Place an empty decanter below the funnel.
- Turn the ON/OFF switch to the ON position.
- Press and release the START switch once. On some models, pressing the START switch twice results in the machine dispensing the correct amount of water twice, resulting in the pot overflowing.
- When brewing is complete, discard the grounds and filter.

FIGURE 5.21 Twin airpot coffee brewer.

Source: Bunn-O-Matic.

Cleaning

URNS   Urns should be thoroughly rinsed after each use by emptying them of all coffee and rinsing them with a gallon of hot water. At the end of the shift, they should be carefully cleaned as follows:

- Remove both funnels, funnel supports, and funnel lids.
- Rinse the funnels, supports, and lids under hot water and wipe them dry with a clean cloth.
- Open both coffee faucets and drain off all coffee. Close the faucets.
- Pour 2 or 3 inches of water into each reservoir. Scrub the entire surface of the reservoirs with an urn brush.
- Drain the reservoirs and rinse them with hot water.
- Wipe down the reservoirs with a clean damp cloth.
- Return the funnels, funnel supports, and funnel lids to their respective places.
- Remove the cap on the top of the sight gauge. Clean the sight glass tube with a sight glass cleaning brush.
- Remove the two coffee urn faucets. (Do not remove the hot water faucet.)
- Clean the reservoir drain with a faucet cleaning brush.
- Remove the faucet handle and clean the faucet with the faucet cleaning brush and a clean damp cloth.
- Reassemble the faucet handle to the faucet and the entire faucet assembly to the urn.
- Clean the exterior of the urn with a clean damp cloth and wipe dry.

DECANTER AND AIRPOT

- Using a damp cloth that has been rinsed in a mild nonabrasive liquid detergent, wipe down all exterior surfaces of the coffee maker.
- Remove the sprayhead and check the holes to ascertain if they are open.
- Clean the sprayhead.
- Insert the de-liming spring into the sprayhead tube until less than 2 inches of the spring is visible. Move the spring back and forth several times.
- Replace the sprayhead.

Maintenance

When cleaning the faucet on urn coffee makers, check the faucet seat cup for wear and replace it if necessary. Periodically de-lime the water tank following the manufacturer's instructions for dilution and use.

Questions

1. Discuss the operational differences between a thermostat and a burner control knob as it applies to electric and gas range tops.
2. Which type of range top would you use for the following applications:

   Sauté

   Stock

   Simmering

   Short-order

   Pan-frying

3. Explain how an induction cooktop works.
4. In your opinion, which griddle top do you prefer? Why?
5. What are the steps taken in cleaning a deep fat fryer? Which is the most important step?
6. Explain how a microwave oven works.
7. Discuss the similarities and differences in a proofing cabinet and a hot holding cabinet.
8. Give the steps in brewing the perfect cup of coffee.

Project

1. Conduct a seminar on gas safety (Chapter 3) and include how to light a gas pilot light. 2. Discuss the advantages and disadvantages of a spark ignition system versus pilot light. 3. Create all your demonstration materials, i.e., flipcharts, posters, power point, etc., on your own.

Acknowledgments

Bunn-O-Matic Corporation, Springfield, IL.
Cres-Cor, Mentor, OH.
Keating of Chicago, Bellwood, IL.

Web Sites

Amana Commercial and Industrial Products Division
www.amanacommercial.com

Blodgett Corporation
www.maytagfoodservice.com

Bunn-O-Matic Corporation
www.bunnmatic.com

Cres-Cor
www.crescor.com

Garland Commercial Ind.
www.garland-group.com

Keating of Chicago
www.keatingofchicago.com

Pitco Fryolator
www.middleby.com

Vulcan-Hart
www.vulcanhart.com

Wolf Range Co.
www.wolfrange.com

Resources

Birchfield, John C. (1998). Design and Layout of Foodservice Facilities. New York, NY: John Wiley & Sons, Inc.

Katsigris, Costas & Thomas, Chris (1999). Design and Equipment for Restaurants and Food-service: A Management View. New York, NY: John Wiley & Sons, Inc.

Kazarian, Edward A. (1997). Foodservice Facilities Planning, 3rd ed. New York, NY: John Wiley & Sons, Inc.

Scriven, C. & Stevens, J. (1982). Food Equipment Facts. New York, NY: John Wiley & Sons, Inc.

Product specification sheets and owners manual from the following companies:

Amana Commercial & Industrial Products Division
Blodgett Corporation
Bunn-O-Matic Corporation
Cres-Cor
Garland Commercial Industries
Keating of Chicago
Pitco Fryolator
Vulcan–Hart
Wolf Range Company

CHAPTER 6

Cooking Equipment Part II

Objectives

Upon completion of this chapter, you will be able to:

- Understand the difference between self-generated and direct source steam equipment.
- Discuss the difference between a conventional oven and a convection oven.
- Identify the various oven styles and the application of each.
- Explain the operation of a pressure steamer.
- Express how a combination oven steamer works and its application in the kitchen.
- Demonstrate the use of a steam-jacketed kettle, explain the different styles, and tell the use of each.
- Discuss the operation of a microwave oven.
- Understand the air removal system in a kitchen, makeup air, and the fire suppressant system.

Key Terms

baffle filter
convection oven
conventional oven
conveyer oven
cook and hold
fire suppressant systems
hood

magnetron
makeup air system
microwave oven
Combination oven steamers
PSI
stationary kettle
steam generator
tilting kettle

INTRODUCTION

This chapter will focus on the several different types of ovens, steam equipment, as well as equipment that combines ovens and steam. The chapter concludes with hoods, ventilation, and fire suppressant systems that have nothing to do with cooking but play an integral role in the operation of cooking equipment.

OVENS

Overview

Many different types and styles of ovens are used in today's kitchens. One point of differentiation is the source of heat. This can be either an electric element or a gas burner, normally located under the oven cavity or deck. A second way to classify them is based on the type of oven, which can be either a conventional oven or a convection oven.

Conventional ovens bake or roast by means of indirect heat coming from the heat source. Heat from the electric element or gas burner rises to the top of the oven cavity, bounces down from and off the sides of the cavity, and indirectly circulates throughout the oven.

Convection ovens, on the other hand, employ the same type of heat source, but a fan blows the air around and throughout the oven cavity. This forced air strips away the layer of cool air that surrounds the product, allowing it to cook more quickly and at a lower temperature. Because of this, care must be exercised when setting the oven thermostat.

The third difference between ovens is based on the various styles:

- Free-standing—Either as a single oven or stacked two or three high, this type comes in the form of either electric or gas, conventional or convection (see Figure 6.1).
- Under-range—Perhaps the most common oven, this type is in use in practically every kitchen. Located under the stove top, it can be either electric or gas, conventional or convection (see Figure 6.2).
- Deck—Single-deck or stacked up to four decks high, deck ovens are primarily used for baking but can also be used for roasting. The heat source can be either electric or gas. Deck ovens are conventional only. Some come with a steam injection option. A variation of the deck oven is the revolving tray oven, sometimes called a reel oven, in which the trays revolve like a Ferris wheel (see Figure 6.3).
- High production oven—In this oven, the product is loaded onto one or two speed racks and rolled directly into the oven. A variation of this is the carousel oven, where the speed rack hooks onto a carousel and the racks turn much like an amusement park carousel (see Figure 6.4).
- Other styles include the conveyer oven, combination bake and steam (combis), and microwave ovens. These three will be covered in detail later in the chapter.

Parts

- Control panel—Contains the ON/OFF switch, the thermostat, the load or preheat light, and if applicable, a timer. On convection ovens, the panel also contains the fan SPEED switch and, if applicable, the fan ON/OFF switch (see Figure 6.5).
- Oven cavity—The inside of the oven where the product is placed.

FIGURE 6.1 Single stack convection oven.

Source: Blodgett.

FIGURE 6.2 Under-range oven.

Source: Vulcan.

- Oven rack—Rack on which the product is placed. Racks are held by a rack support and most ovens contain several racks.
- Heating elements—Either gas burner or electric rod.
- Interior light—Lights the interior of the oven to observe the product without opening the oven door and cooling down the oven cavity.
- Blower wheel—(convection oven only) The fan that circulates the hot air throughout the oven (see Figure 6.6).

Operation

For under-range ovens, free-standing ovens, and deck ovens of both conventional and convection types, follow these guidelines.

FIGURE 6.3 Deck oven.

Source: Garland.

FIGURE 6.4   Roll-in oven.

Source: Blodgett.

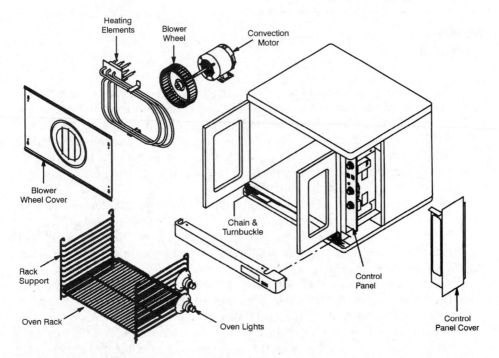

FIGURE 6.5   Convection oven control panel.

Source: Blodgett.

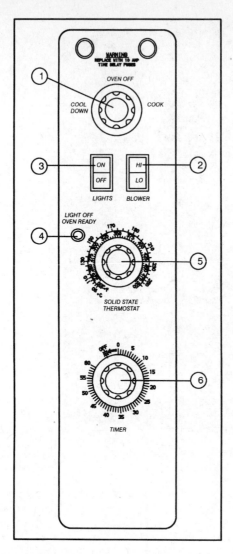

CONTROL DESCRIPTION

1. SELECTOR SWITCH—controls power to the oven for cook or cool down.
2. BLOWER SWITCH—controls blower speed, either hi or lo.
3. LIGHTS SWITCH—controls interior lights.
4. OVEN READY LIGHT—when lit indicates burner operation. When the light goes out the oven has reached operating temperature.
5. SOLID STATE THERMOSTAT—allows either 8 pre-set temperatures to be selected in accordance with customer requirements, or an infinite selection of temperatures from 200 to 500°F (95–260°C) (infinite control shown).
6. TIMER—activates an electric buzzer that sounds when the cook time expires.

OPERATION

1. Turn the SELECTOR Switch (1) to *COOK*. The blower and control compartment cooling fan operate and are controlled automatically by the action of the doors.
2. Set BLOWER Switch (2) to the desired speed.
3. Set the SOLID STATE THERMOSTAT (5) to the desired setting or temperature.
4. Preheat until the OVEN READY LIGHT (4) goes out.
5. Load product into the oven. Determine cook time and set the TIMER (6).
6. When the buzzer sounds, remove the product from the oven. Turn the TIMER knob (6) to *OFF* to silence the buzzer.
7. Turn the SELECTOR Switch (1) to *OVEN OFF*.

FIGURE 6.6 Parts of a convection oven.

Source: Blodgett.

1. Preheat the oven—Always preheat the oven to the temperature at which you are going to bake or roast. Some manufacturers recommend preheating the oven 50°F (10°C) above the intended temperature. This compensates for the drop in temperature while the doors are open and cold product is loaded into the oven. After placing the product in the oven, reduce the thermostat to the proper temperature. Some ovens are equipped with a preheat option that automatically handles this function.

2. Set the temperature—If using a conventional oven, set the temperature as the recipe dictates. If using a convection oven, the temperature should be set 50°F (10°C) lower than for a conventional oven, as the forced air will compensate for the lower temperature. The product should bake or roast in the same amount of time as for a conventional oven. Check the product. If at the end of the estimated cooking time it is done around the edges, but not in the center, reduce the thermostat another 15–25°F (10–15°C). When setting temperatures, be careful. Thermostats are not always exact. Temperature and cooking time will also be affected by the amount of product, the size and type of pan used, and the temperature of the product going into the oven.

3. Load the oven—Always load the oven from the bottom up. Center the pan(s) on the rack. If only one pan is to be used, place it on the center rack. Be sure

that the product is distributed evenly if several pans are being used. If baking, weigh the pans to ensure equal distribution that will in turn ensure equal baking time. Never place a pan or aluminum foil on the bottom of the oven. While this facilitates cleanup, it affects the distribution of heat in the oven and, in the case of convection ovens, restricts the movement of air. After loading the oven, set the timer. *Note:* Unlike some other pieces of equipment, the timer does not control the oven. When the timer goes off, the oven continues to operate until it is physically turned off.

4a. Conventional oven operation

- Turn the power switch to ON. On some models this is called COOK.
- Set the thermostat to the desired temperature.
- Preheat the oven to the desired temperature. On some models, a light will come on, indicating that the oven is ready to be loaded, while on other models, a preheat light will go off when the oven is ready.
- Load the oven.
- If the oven is equipped with a timer, set it for the desired time.
- When the product is done, remove the pan(s), turn the thermostat to zero, and turn the power switch to OFF.

4b. Convection oven operation

The operation for a convection oven, for the most part, is the same as for a conventional oven. The two exceptions are the fan and the temperature setting. On most models, the fan goes on when the door is shut. The only option is the fan speed, which can be selected as high or low. Some models have an option as to whether the fan is on or off. If the fan is off, the oven reverts to being a conventional oven. Regarding temperature, if the oven is being operated as a convection oven, remember to reduce the thermostat 50°F (10°C).

4c. Cook and hold cycle

Some ovens come equipped with an optional cook and hold cycle. The operation is similar to a convection oven operation. There is an additional thermostat and timer on the control panel called the hold thermostat and the cook and hold timer.

- Preheat the oven by turning the power ON and setting the cook thermostat to the desired temperature.
- When it reaches the proper temperature, place the product in the oven.
- Set the HOLD thermostat to the temperature at which you want the product to be held.
- Set the COOK & HOLD timer for the amount of time the product is to be cooked.
- Turn the power switch to COOK & HOLD.

When the cook time expires on the cook and hold timer, the oven reduces its temperature to that indicated on the hold thermostat. The oven stays at this temperature until the product is removed and the oven is turned OFF. On some models, when the oven goes from the cook cycle to the hold cycle, the fan goes off and comes back on only when the burner or heating element comes on.

Cleaning

Most oven cavity interiors are made of porcelain and can be cleaned using a commercial-grade oven cleaner. Carefully follow the manufacturer's directions when using the product. Use insulated gloves, safety goggles, and a heat-resistant apron when cleaning. Prior to cleaning, remove the oven racks, rack supports, and the blower wheel from the oven. Clean these parts by soaking them in a solution of ammonia and water. The blower wheel and the panel behind it are normally made out of aluminized steel and should not come into contact with the oven cleaner or any other caustic cleaning compound. The exterior finish can be kept clean by saturating a cloth with light oil and wiping the oven. If the exterior is stainless steel, a stainless steel cleaner may be used. Always apply cleaner and oil when the oven is cold.

Maintenance

On gas ovens the flame should be checked periodically to make sure that it is burning blue. If there is any yellow in the flame, it should be adjusted by an authorized technician. Additionally, the venting system should be checked annually by an authorized representative for possible deterioration from moisture and corrosive flue products.

CONVEYER OVEN

Overview

The **conveyer oven**, sometimes referred to by a brand name, "Impinger oven," has a limited use in the kitchen. While it can be used to bake cookies, pies, and other items, its primary use has evolved into baking pizzas. It is almost foolproof to operate (keeping in mind that no equipment is totally foolproof). A conveyor belt carries the product through the oven cavity. The product is placed on the belt on the loading end and comes out fully baked on the receiving end. The speed of the belt determines the length of time that the product is in the oven. It is a form of convection oven in that a fan blows hot air on the product. Its heating source is either electric or gas (see Figure 6.7).

Parts

Conveyer drive motor—Moves the conveyer belt.

End trays—Catches the product as it exits the oven at the receiving end (see Figure 6.8, A).

Conveyer—Moves the product through the oven at a predetermined rate which allows the product to be in the oven for a specified period of time (B).

Crumb pans—Catches crumbs and other things that fall through the conveyer belt.

Control panel—Houses the operating controls for the oven (C) (see also Figure 6.9).

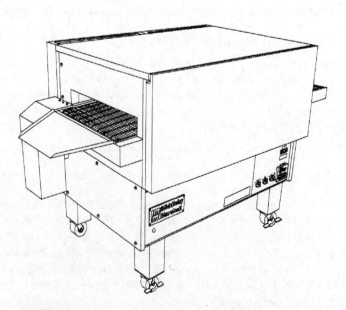

FIGURE 6.7

Source: Blodgett.

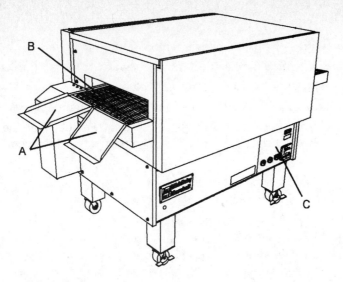

FIGURE 6.8 Conveyor oven parts.

Source: Blodgett.

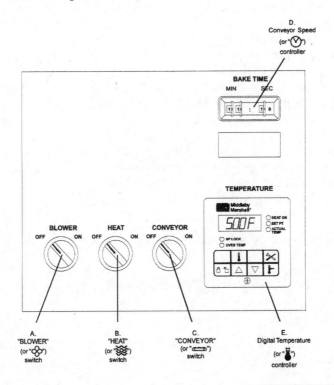

 A.

"BLOWER" Switch: Turns the blowers and cooling fans on and off. The HEAT Switch has no effect unless the BLOWER Switch is in the "ON" position.

B. **"HEAT" Switch:** Allows the gas burner to light. Activation of the gas burner is determined by the settings on the Digital Temperature Controller.

C. **"CONVEYOR" Switch:** Turns the conveyor drive motor on and off.

D. **Conveyor Speed Controller:** Adjusts and displays the bake time.

E. **Digital Temperature Controller:** Continuously monitors the oven temperature. Settings on the Digital Temperture Controller control the activation of the gas burner.

NOT SHOWN:

F. **Machinery Compartment Access Panel Safety Switch:** Disconnects electrical power to the controls and the blowers when the machinery compartment access panel is opened. The panel should only be opened by authorized service personnel.

FIGURE 6.9 Conveyor oven control panel.

Source: Blodgett.

Blower switch—Turns the blower fan on or off.

Heat switch—Turns the electrical heating element or the gas burners on or off.

Conveyer switch—Turns the conveyer belt on or off.

Temperature gauge—A digital readout of the oven temperature.

Conveyer speed control—Allows for setting the speed of the conveyer, which determines the amount of time the product is in the oven.

Operation

Most conveyer ovens operate in a similar manner:

- Switch the circuit breaker to the ON position.
- Turn the blower switch to the ON position.
- Turn the conveyer switch to the ON position.
- Adjust the conveyer speed setting. Normally this is expressed in minutes and seconds, denoting the amount of time that the product on the conveyer is in the oven cavity.
- Adjust the temperature setting to the desired temperature.
- Turn the heat switch to the ON position. Most ovens have a light indicating that the heat is on.
- Wait for the oven to come to the desired temperature. This will normally take approximately 5–10 minutes.
- When the oven has reached the proper temperature, place the product on the conveyer on the loading end. Check the product on the receiving end for proper doneness. If necessary, make adjustments on the temperature or the conveyer speed.
- At the end of the shift, reverse the procedure to shut the oven down. The blowers will continue to operate until the oven has cooled down.
- Switch the circuit breaker to the OFF position.

Cleaning

Prior to cleaning the oven, make sure that it has cooled down and that the circuit breaker is in the OFF position.

When cleaning the oven, do not use a water hose, pressurized steam cleaning equipment, or an excessive amount of water. Also do not use any caustic oven cleaners.

When the oven has cooled down:

- Remove the panels and clean the cooling fan grills and vents using a stiff nylon brush.
- Replace the panels.
- Turn the circuit breaker and the conveyer ON.
- Clean the conveyer with a stiff nylon brush at the receiving end of the oven as the conveyer moves. When complete, turn the conveyer off and switch the circuit breaker to the OFF position.
- Remove and clean the crumb trays and replace.
- Clean the exterior of the oven using a cloth dampened with a solution of mild detergent and water.

Maintenance

Since maintenance requires that the oven be disassembled, it is recommended that a qualified service technician perform the following maintenance procedures.

- Monthly—Remove the air finger components. Clean the air finger components and the interior of the oven using a damp cloth and a vacuum cleaner (see Figure 6.10).
- Quarterly—Vacuum the blower motors and compartments.

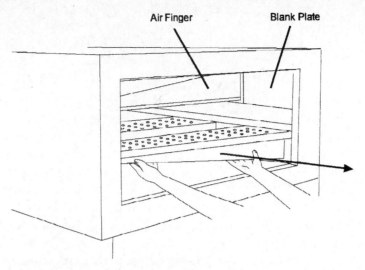

FIGURE 6.10 Removing the air finger components.
Source: Blodgett.

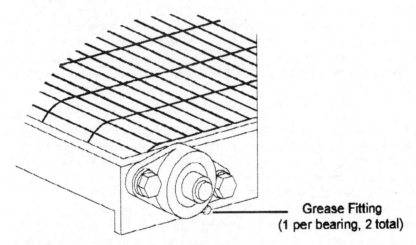

FIGURE 6.11 Grease fitting for lubrication.
Source: Blodgett.

- Semiannually—Check and, if necessary, replace the conveyer drive motor brushings. Clean the burner nozzle, electrode assembly, the oven venting system, and the flue. Check and replace, if necessary, the conveyer drive shaft bushing and spacers.
- Annually—Lubricate the drive shaft bearings (see Figure 6.11).

MICROWAVE OVEN

Overview

Microwave ovens are unusual in that they enjoy a love/hate relationship in the kitchen. Some foodservice operations can't get along without them and in others they sit there unused. As a matter of fact, some chefs have even banned them from their kitchens. While microwaves are not a cure-all for every cooking situation, they do have their place. They do well in reheating products from the frozen or chilled state. They are excellent for quickly thawing products. They are also very good in cooking fresh or frozen vegetables. Microwave ovens should not be used for cooking meats since they tend to toughen the product and do not do a good job of browning the outer surface of the meat. They also should not be

FIGURE 6.12
Source: Amana.

used for baking unless the product or mix has been especially formulated for microwave baking (see Figure 6.12).

Microwave ovens do not cook product through heat transfer like an electrical rod or gas flame. Rather a **magnetron** sends waves of radiation into the food where they agitate molecules of water. The agitation causes friction, which in turn creates heat, which in turn cooks the food. Thus, the food becomes the heat source. Since the radiation penetrates only a few inches into the product, when large portions of food are placed in the microwave, the heat generated by the molecular motion at the surface is transferred into the product by conduction. In other words, if a roast were placed in the microwave, the outer inch or two would be heated (cooked) by the molecular motion. The portion further inside the roast would be cooked by heat transferred from the outer part.

Two things become readily apparent.

1. The food must have moisture content—The higher the moisture content, the quicker the cooking process. Objects with no moisture content will not cook via the microwave process but could become hot via heat being conducted into them. For example, microwaves cook the food placed on a plate, but the plate, with no water content, is heated by heat transfer from the food.
2. Smaller pieces cook quicker—Microwave cooking is designed for small-batch cooking. While it will work on larger portions, it looses its effectiveness for speed.

Therefore, small quantities with high moisture content work best. As moisture decreases and size increases, the effectiveness of the microwave decreases.

Another fact to consider regarding the speed of cooking is the wattage of the microwave oven. The higher the wattage, the quicker the product cooks. Most commercial microwaves come in 650, 1,000, or 1,400 watts. It is important to know the wattage of the oven you are using because cooking times will differ. A small potato will cook in four minutes in a 650-watt oven, while the same potato will cook in three minutes in a 1,000-watt oven.

Parts

- Control panel—Contains the ON/OFF or START/STOP switch; timer; power level; and on some models, specific buttons for specific menu items.
- Door—Contains a mechanical interlock to prevent the microwave from being turned on unless the door is securely closed. Also has a window that is designed to keep the radiation in the oven cavity while letting the operator observe the food cooking.
- Oven cavity—The area in which the food is placed.

Operation

The best instruction as to how to operate a microwave oven is to read the owner's manual. There are so many differences that it is impossible to cover them in this section. First, there is the control panel. Some operate with a manual dial, some have a keypad, and others have a computerized digital touch pad. Some microwaves operate with a timer only, while others have individual settings for specific menu items. On most models with specific settings, these can be changed to suit the user's requirements. As mentioned earlier, several different wattages are available, which affect the cooking time. The time that works on your microwave at home for a specific item is not necessarily the same time you would use on the oven at work.

Given all the variables, a few constant factors apply to most ovens.

- Place the product to be microwaved in the oven cavity, close the door securely, select the time, select the power level, and turn the oven on.
- Another constant among microwaves is the selection of power level. Most microwaves allow you to select a power level from 0 percent (no power) to 100 percent (full power) in increments of 10. For example, 80 percent power is used for reheating and 30 percent power is used for defrosting. A few basic models have no power settings and go on 100 percent power all the time.
- Because microwaves work with radiation and work very quickly, more "don'ts" than "do's" are involved with its use.
  - Don't tamper with the safety interlock and allow the microwave to operate with the door open. This can result in harmful exposure to microwave energy.
  - Don't operate the oven if the door is damaged, if the hinges or latches are broken, or if the door seals are cracked. Do not allow soil to accumulate on the door seals.
  - Don't operate the oven without food or liquid in the oven cavity.
  - Don't use regular cooking thermometers in the oven since they contain mercury and could cause an electrical arc.
  - Don't use metal utensils in the oven.
  - Don't heat baby bottles in the oven.
  - Don't place heat-sealed containers or plastic bags in the oven without first piercing or opening the bag. Don't cook product in sealed jars.
  - Don't deep fat fry in the oven since the fat could overheat and cause a fire.
  - Don't cook eggs in the microwave without first piercing the yolk of the egg.
  - Don't cook potatoes, tomatoes, or other vegetable with a skin without first piercing the skin to allow steam to escape.
  - Don't use paper, plastic, or other combustible material that is not intended for cooking; a fire could occur. Should a fire occur, keep the door to the unit closed, turn the unit off, and disconnect the power cord.

One more thing: Some pacemakers are affected by microwave ovens. To avoid possible malfunction, consult the manufacturer of the pacemaker or a physician.

Cleaning

Clean the microwave oven regularly, preferably after every use. Residue left in the oven cavity will continue to cook. Not only will this reduce the efficiency of the oven by cooking the residue, but it will harden with each subsequent use and become more difficult to clean. Additionally, grease or fat could ignite and cause a fire. Prior to cleaning the oven, make sure it is unplugged. To clean the oven, use a soft sponge or cloth that has been soaked in a solution of mild detergent and water. Wring the sponge or cloth to remove all excess water and wipe the interior and exterior of the oven. If an excessive amount of hardened soil is in the oven, boil a cup of water to loosen the soil and then clean. Do not use any abrasive cleansers or cleaners containing ammonia.

Maintenance

Most microwave ovens come equipped with an air filter. On a weekly basis, remove the air filter according to the manufacturer's directions and clean it with a solution of mild detergent and water. Never operate the oven without the filter (see Figure 6.13).

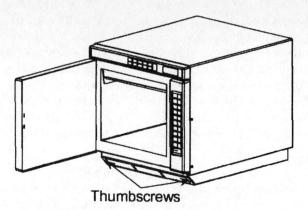

Thumbscrews

FIGURE 6.13 The vent under the oven must be removed to locate the filter. While the filter is located under the oven on most models, check your manufacturer's directions.

Source: Amana.

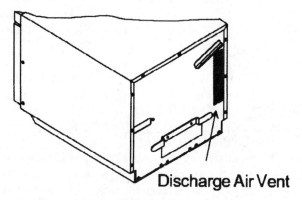

Discharge Air Vent

FIGURE 6.14 The discharge air vent is located behind the oven on most models.

Source: Amana.

On a monthly basis, check the discharge louvers that are normally located in the back of the oven and clean them with a damp cloth, then dry thoroughly (see Figure 6.14).

STEAM EQUIPMENT

Steam source A commonality of all steam equipment is the source of steam. It can come from three sources: a central steam plant, a boiler, or a steam generator.

1. Central steam—Steam can come from a central plant in two scenarios. First, in many large cities, steam can be purchased much like electricity, gas, or water. Steam is produced in a central plant and goes underground in pipes to buildings within the city. The primary use of this steam is to heat the buildings, but it can also be directed to the kitchen where it can be hooked up to the steam equipment. The second scenario involves a large complex of buildings, such as a college campus, prison, or office complex, where a central plant supplies steam to all the buildings within the complex.
2. Boiler—The boiler could be within the building housing the foodservice operation. Again, the primary purpose of the steam from the boiler is to heat the building, but, as in the case of the central plant, this steam can also be used for the kitchen equipment.
3. Steam generator—This steam source is built into the equipment and is used in operations where a direct steam source is not available. Steam-jacketed

kettles use chemically pure water that contains rust inhibitors, while pressure steamers and oven steamers use regular tap water. The water is heated in the generator to produce steam. With the self-contained unit, the heat source that creates the steam can be either electric or gas. While some of the large industrial or institutional kitchens use direct steam, most of today's operations use self-generated steam equipment.

PRESSURE STEAMER

Overview

Pressure steamers do just what their name implies. They steam food under pressure. Used properly, they can cook a product quickly while retaining its color, texture, and nutrients. Unless the kitchen has a central steam source, the pressure steamer produces its own steam in a steam generator. Since this generator uses regular tap water, the maintenance of this unit is very important. Lime and other mineral deposits can form and slow down or even stop the production of steam. How to prevent and/or correct this is covered in the maintenance part of this section.

The steam is circulated throughout the steamer cavity by means of a fan. Excess steam and condensate escape through the drain pipe, which discharges into an open floor drain in the kitchen. This should be located at the back of the unit and away from any foot traffic (see Figure 6.15).

Parts

- Power switch—Turns the unit on or off.
- Timer—Sets the amount of time that the unit will be on. When the unit is set at the ON position, it operates continuously until it is manually turned off.
- Ready light—Indicates that the unit has created steam and is ready to operate.
- Service light (on some units called the cleaning light)—Indicates that the steamer needs to be delimed.
- Steamer cavity—The area where the product is placed to be steamed (see Figure 6.16).

FIGURE 6.15
Source: Cleveland.

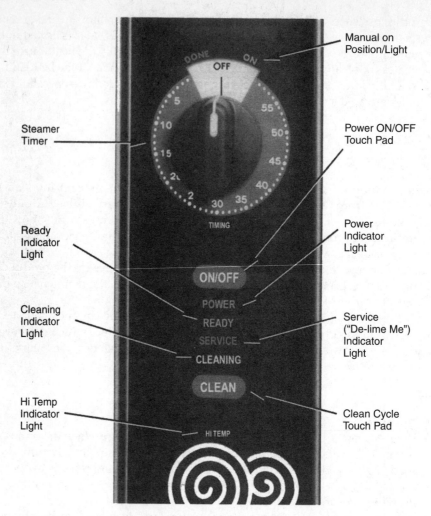

FIGURE 6.16 Control panel for a pressure steamer.

Source: Groen.

Operation

- Since most steamers generate their own steam, turn the unit to the ON position about ten minutes prior to cooking. When the unit is turned on, the steam generator fills with water, which heats up until steam is formed.
- When this occurs, the READY light comes on and the unit is set for use.
- Load the food into the pan(s) in uniform layers. Most steamers are built to take full, half, or third size steam table pans and can go directly from the pressure steamer to the steam table. The food should be level on top. If more than one pan is being steamed at the same time, each pan should contain the same amount of product and be filled to the same level. Slide the pan(s) onto the supports in the steamer cavity. If only one pan is to be steamed, load it in the middle position.
- Close the door.
- Turn the steamer on. There are two options in operating the steamer. One is to set the timer for the desired amount of cooking time. The steamer then operates for that amount of time and automatically shuts off. When this occurs, a bell or buzzer sounds. The second option is to set the timer control knob to the ON position. With this option, the steamer operates continuously until the timer control knob is turned to the OFF position.

- When the product is properly steamed, stand to the side of the oven and open the door. Using hot pads or oven mitts, carefully remove the pan(s) from the steamer cavity.
- Turn the unit off by switching the power ON/OFF switch to the OFF position.

Cleaning

Clean the interior of the steamer cavity by using a solution of mild detergent and water and a clean cloth. Wait at least five minutes after turning the steamer off to allow it to cool. Make sure that the fan has shut off prior to cleaning. To remove any product that has adhered to the side of the cavity, use a brush or plastic scraper. Check that the drain holes at the back of the cavity are clear of any debris.

To clean the exterior of the pressure steamer, first disconnect the power supply. Keep water and cleaning solutions out of and away from the control panel and any electrical components. Do not hose down or steam clean any part of the unit. Use a solution of warm water and mild detergent to wipe down the exterior of the unit. The exterior can then be polished with a stainless steel cleaner and polish if desired. On both the exterior and the interior cavity, do not use any metal material such as a spatula, wire brush, steel wool, or metal sponge.

Maintenance

Two maintenance items need to be taken care of on an as-needed basis.

STEAM GENERATOR   Most water supplies contain minerals that form scale. Scale formation in the steam generator is the major cause of unit failure. To slow down scale formation, use of a water softener is highly recommended. Even with a water softener, it is necessary from time to time to de-lime the unit.

When a slowdown in steam production is noticed, it's time to check the unit. Some models come equipped with a warning light that indicates when a unit is in need of de-liming. When de-liming a unit, do not allow the de-liming agent to come into contact with any degreasers.

To de-lime the pressure steamer:

1. Turn the ON/OFF switch to the OFF position.
2. Turn the timer knob to the OFF position.
3. Open the door and allow the cavity to cool for five minutes.
4. Remove the fan baffle by lifting it up and toward the center of the cavity.
5. Using a funnel, pour two cups of de-limer into the de-limer port. Do not use a de-limer that contains chlorine.
6. Turn the steamer to the ON position and turn the timer to ten minutes.
7. After the unit has shut off and cooled, replace the fan baffle partition.
8. After ten minutes, close the door, turn the power switch to the ON position, and set the timer for ten minutes to flush out the steam generator tank.
9. At the end of this process, turn the steamer to the OFF position, open the door, and wipe out the cavity of the steamer. It is now ready for use.

Some manufacturers and/or models have an automated cleaning and de-liming cycle. In this case follow the directions in the operator's manual (see Figure 6.17).

DOOR GASKET   If steam or condensate is leaking from around the door, the gasket probably needs adjusting or replacing. Before that is done, however, check to see if the drain in the steamer cavity is blocked, which could also cause leakage. Check the gasket for cracks or splits. If it has either, it needs to be replaced. If the gasket is okay and the drain is not blocked, adjust the latch pin. First, loosen the lock nut at the base of the latch pin. Turn the latch pin a quarter turn clockwise and retighten the lock nut. Test the unit. If leakage still occurs, repeat the adjustments until the door fits tight.

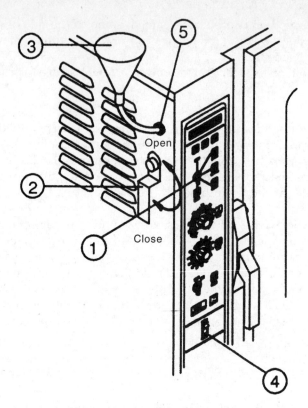

FIGURE 6.17 Parts of the de-liming procedure include (1) de-liming switch, (2) de-liming valve, (3) funnel, (4) power switch, (5) de-liming hole.

Source: Blodgett.

COMBINATION OVEN STEAMERS

Overview

Popularly called combis, the oven steamer is an answer to the foodservice industry's call for more efficient use of space in the kitchen as well as a more efficient use of capital. Thus, what once was two pieces of equipment is now one. While industry was slow to embrace the combi, in recent years more and more of them have been purchased and today practically every major kitchen has one (see Figure 6.18).

A combi can be used as an oven to bake or roast, it can be used as a steamer to steam products or it can do both, either together (roast and steam) or in sequence (roast then steam or steam then roast). It is excellent for reheating precooked products and convenience foods. Most frozen food can be processed without pre-thawing, thus eliminating product being in the danger zone. All combi's have a minimum of three cooking modes:

- Oven mode: The oven steamer has an electric heating element or a gas burner that is used when the equipment is in the oven form of operation. It has a fan that circulates the air throughout the oven cavity and is thus operated as a convection oven. This mode is used for roasting or baking.
- Steamer mode: Works like a steamer and is used for blanching, steaming, and simmering. As we all know, gently steaming vegetables retains their nutritional value over other methods of cookery. An interesting aside is that different foods can be placed in the combi and steamed at the same time with no transfer of flavor from one food to the other. In most units, a steam generator is built into the unit that takes tap water and generates it into steam. In those kitchens with direct steam, the unit does not have a generator and receives its steam from a central boiler. A fan circulates the steam throughout the oven cavity. There is a

FIGURE 6.18
Source: Cleveland.

condenser that draws out excess steam from the unit and a drain to remove condensation and wastewater.

- Combination mode: Uses both the convection oven and the steamer. This mode cooks food up to 50 percent faster. When roasting, the need for basting is eliminated and product shrinkage is reduced 20–30 percent. It can also be used for baking hard-crusted breads. With the steam injection, products come out evenly browned.

In addition to the three standard modes, optional features can be added such as:

- Varied steam: Injects steam intermittently, rather than constantly.
- Steam on demand: The user manually injects steam with a push button.
- Roast and hold: The product has a probe inserted and when a predetermined internal temperature is reached, the oven goes from a roasting function to a holding function.
- Slow cooking: This mode roasts at low temperatures. Check with local authorities to see if this feature is approved in your jurisdiction.
- Gentle steaming: Used for delicate foods such as fish.
- Crisper: De-moisturizes food for a crisp texture.

Parts

- Control panel—Contains the ON/OFF touch pad, the cooking mode selection touch pad, the timer, the thermostat, the display window, and on some models the humidity control.
- Cooking chamber—the interior of the oven, the same thing as an oven cavity, normally constructed out of stainless steel.
- Fan—circulates the air when the oven mode is on, much like a convection oven.
- Hose assembly—Used to clean the unit.
- **Steam generator**—produces steam when the unit is in the steam or combi mode. If direct steam is available, the unit will not have a generator (see Figure 6.19).

Operation

As mentioned, there are three different forms of operation on the oven steamer. The hot air form of operation is used to roast, bake, and braise. The steam form of operation is used to steam, defrost, blanch, and poach. The combination form of operation is used to defrost, reheat, roast, and bake; some models have optional controls such as proof, **cook and hold**, and sous vide. While most oven-steamers operate as follows, there could be some minor differences in your particular unit.

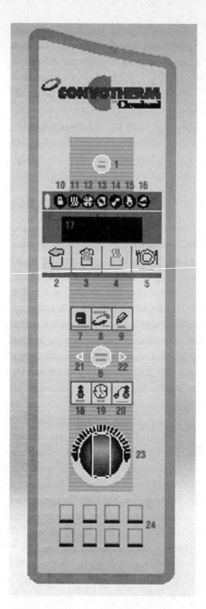

FIGURE 6.19 An example of a control panel on a combination oven steamer.

Source: Cleveland.

OVEN MODE To use the unit as an oven, follow these instructions:

- Turn the unit ON.
- Select the OVEN or HOT AIR mode.
- Select the desired temperature. Note that this is a convection oven; hence, the temperature should be set accordingly.
- When the unit is properly heated the READY light will come on.
- Load the product evenly into pan(s).
- Load the pan(s) into the oven. If only one pan is being used, load it onto the middle rack.
- Set the cooking time. *Note:* Unlike the steamer that shuts the unit down when the time has expired, in the oven mode, the unit will continue to operate even after the time has expired.
- Press START.
- When the product is done, turn the unit off. Again, the timer will not automatically shut the unit off.
- Using hot pads, remove the pan(s).

STEAMER MODE   To use the unit as a steamer, follow these instructions:

- Turn the unit ON.
- Select the STEAM mode.
- When the unit is properly heated the READY light will come on.
- Load the product evenly into pan(s).
- Load the pan(s) into the steamer.
- Set the cooking time.
- Press START.
- When the timer reaches zero, the steaming process will stop.
- Open the door carefully, standing to the side to avoid escaping steam.
- Using hot pads, remove the pans.

COMBINATION MODE   To use the unit as a combination oven steamer, follow these instructions:

- Turn the unit ON.
- Select the COMBI or COMBO mode.
- Select the desired temperature.
- When the unit is properly heated, the READY light will come on.
- Load the product evenly into pan(s).
- Load the pan(s) into the oven. If only one pan is being used, load it onto the middle rack.
- Set the cooking time. *Note:* Unlike the steamer that shuts the unit down when the time has expired, in the combo mode, the unit will continue to operate after the time has expired. The combo mode can be run without the timer.
- Press START.
- When the product is done, turn the unit off. Again, the timer will not automatically shut the unit off.
- Using hot pads, remove the pan(s).

Cleaning

CLEANING THE INTERIOR   The interior cavity of the oven steamer can be cleaned either with the racks, rack supporters, and blower wheel in place or they can be removed. If the oven steamer has a standard finish on the interior cavity and is being cleaned immediately after use, cool the interior down to 140°F (60°C). If the unit has been off for a while, warm it up by turning on the steam mode for three to four minutes.

- Spray the interior cavity with an oven-cleaning detergent. Do not use any corrosive cleaners. Do not spray the interior if the temperature is above 212°F (100°C).
- Let the cleaning detergent work for 20 minutes. The unit should be OFF during this procedure. For extra tough stains, allow it to work overnight.
- Set the timer for 20 minutes and turn the selector switch to STEAM. This will soften any residue in the cavity.
- When the steamer goes off, rinse the interior with the attached hose and spray assembly.
- Finally, set the selector switch to STEAM for five more minutes to flush out any detergent residue.

If the interior of the oven steamer is stainless steel, it can be cleaned with a nontoxic industrial strength stainless steel cleaner. The oven steamer should be cold. Spray the cleaner on and wipe it with the grain of the stainless steel with a clean cloth. Read and follow the manufacturer's directions for this procedure.

CLEANING THE EXTERIOR   The exterior of the oven steamer may be cleaned with a stainless steel polish. Do not spray the exterior of the unit with water.

Maintenance

The primary maintenance to be performed on an oven steamer is the de-liming process and this is only if the unit has its own steam generator (Which most do). Follow these steps to de-lime the unit:

- Turn the selection switch to STEAM. Wait until steam is produced.
- Turn the selection switch to COOL DOWN. Open the doors and let the oven cool to 150°F (66°C).
- Turn the selection switch to OFF.
- Mix the de-liming solution with hot tap water according to the manufacturers directions. The amount needed will vary by the capacity of the steam generator but will usually fall in the 3-quart to 3-gallon range.
- Remove the de-liming port cap from the de-liming inlet and attach the funnel and hose assembly.
- Open the de-liming port valve and pour in the de-liming mixture until the funnel stops draining.
- Shut the de-liming port valve and screw on the de-liming port cap. Let the mixture stand for 20 minutes. If the water in your area is particularly hard, let it stand for one hour.
- Depress and hold the drain/flush switch in the FLUSH position for 90 seconds.
- The de-liming process is now complete.

STEAM-JACKETED KETTLES

Overview

Between a wide range of manufacturers and models, there are many variations of steam-jacketed kettles. However, they all work on the same premise. An enclosed steam jacket covers the sides and bottom of the kettle. Steam circulates throughout this jacket and cooks the product. The pressure of the steam is measured in PSI (pounds per square inch). The **PSI** at which the unit operates varies among kettles. This information can usually be found on the kettle on the information nameplate.

Steam kettles are quite efficient, because the heat source is on the bottom and the sides of the product simultaneously. This is opposed to a stove top, where the heat source is on the bottom only and much of the heat from the source is dissipated into the air. Thus, products can cook quicker in a steam-jacketed kettle with a minimal loss of heat.

Now, for the variations:

- The steam can be directly infused into the steam jacket, or it can come from a self-contained unit.
- Another variation is the variety of the jacket. It can either be a full jacket, two-thirds, or a half. The steam circulates throughout the jacket and the jacket either comes half way up the side of the kettle, two-thirds of the way, or all the way to the top of the kettle.
- The kettle can be either stationary or tilting. On a stationary kettle, the product is removed either manually or through a draw-off valve (drain) at the bottom of the kettle (see Figure 6.20). **Tilting kettles**, on the other hand, tip forward and the product is drawn off into a storage container (see Figure 6.21). Typically, **stationary kettles** are used for liquids such as stocks, and tilting kettles are used for more solid products such as stews.
- One last variation is that steam-jacketed kettles can be either floor-mounted, which are larger-capacity units, or table-mounted, which are smaller-capacity units (see Figure 6.22).

Parts

- ON/OFF switch—Controls the power to the unit.
- Thermostat—Sets and controls the cooking temperature.

FIGURE 6.20   Floor-mounted stationary steam-jacketed kettle.

Source: Groen.

- Water gauge glass—Shows the level of the water within the steam jacket.
- Pressure/vacuum gauge—Shows the steam pressure and if there is air in the jacket.
- Indicator lamp—Light is on when the kettle is being heated.
- Safety valve—Releases steam if the jacket pressure gets too high.
- Draw-off valve—A drain at the bottom of a stationary kettle that allows the product to be removed from the kettle. (See Figure 6.23 for the various parts of steam-jacketed kettle.)

FIGURE 6.21   Floor-mounted tilting steam-jacketed kettle.

Source: Groen.

FIGURE 6.22 Table model steam-jacketed kettle.

Source: Groen.

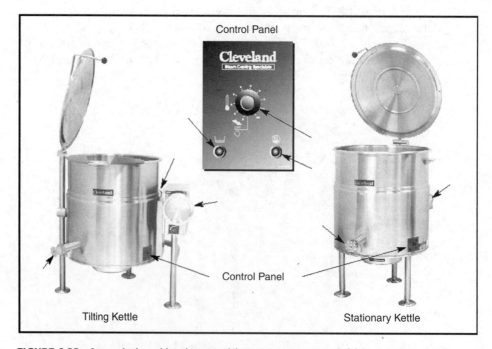

FIGURE 6.23 Steam-jacketed kettle parts. (1) temperature control, (2) heat indicator light, (3) low water indicator light, (4) pressure gauge, (5) pressure relief valve, (6) tilt wheel, (7) power tilt control switch (not shown), (8) drain-off valve.

Source: Cleveland.

Operation

- Prior to cooking product in a steam-jacketed kettle, check the water level in the jacket by looking at the gauge glass and ascertaining that the water level is between the maximum and minimum level.
- Check the pressure gauge while the unit is cold. It should be between 20 and 30 digits below the zero marking. If there is a positive reading or if the reading is near zero, then there is air in the jacket and the unit will not operate properly. Consult the maintenance section below for instructions on how to remedy this.
- If the kettle is stationary, make sure that the strainer is properly placed over the draw-off outlet at the bottom of the kettle and that the valve is closed.
- Place the product to be cooked or the medium in which the product is to be cooked (i.e., oil for braising or water for pasta) into the unit.
- Turn the power switch to ON.
- Turn the thermostat to the desired temperature. (Check the recipe for the proper temperature.)
- If the kettle does not come on and it is a gas unit, check the main gas valve to be sure that it is in the ON position. If it is a standing pilot light kettle, check to be sure the pilot light is on. If it is not, refer to Chapter 5 for instructions on how to light the pilot. If the kettle is electric, make sure that the breaker is in the ON position in the circuit breaker box.
- Do not overload the kettle. Keep liquids at least 3 inches (8 centimeters) below the rim of the kettle to avoid having the product splash out when it is stirred or comes to the boiling point. Allow for displacement when adding additional product later, such as pasta to boiling water.
- Some units come with an optional cover. When placing the cover on the kettle, position it on top of the rim of the kettle with its flat edge facing the pouring lip. When removing the cover, lift the rear edge of the cover slightly to let steam and water escape, waiting a second to allow any condensation to roll off back into the kettle.
- To turn the unit off, first turn the thermostat to OFF and then press the power switch to OFF.
- To empty the kettle:
  - Stationary kettle—Stationary units can be emptied in three ways:
    1. The first and the most tedious is to physically ladle the product out. Since this is very time-consuming, personnel would be better utilized by using a tilting skillet if one is available in the kitchen.
    2. The second method is to drain the product off using the draw-off valve. Make sure the vessel that the product is being transferred to is on a flat, level surface.
    3. The third method is to use a basket insert. This is used for such items as eggs, vegetables, shellfish, or pastas. When removing the cooked product, lift the basket straight up, making sure that the basket clears the rim of the kettle. Allow the hot water to drain completely from the basket before moving it away from the kettle. If the basket is heavy, get help in moving it. *Note:* Always wear an oven mitt and a protective apron when removing product from the kettle.
  - Tilting kettle—When emptying a tilting kettle:
    Grasp the ball of the handle firmly and slowly pull the handle forward. The product comes out of the pouring lip at the front of the kettle. If the handle is pulled too quickly, the product splashes out over the pouring lip and may not go into the intended storage container. This could cause a severe burn.
    Make sure the container that the product is being drained into is on a flat level surface and is stable.
    When draining product, stand to the side of the kettle to avoid being splashed and always wear oven mitts and a protective apron.

After the kettle is emptied, return it to its original position by pushing the ball of the handle backward.

Note: On some older models, a spring-loaded latch locks the handle in place when the kettle is tilted. To release this lock, pull up on the handle and move the kettle forward or backward. Some larger models have a hand wheel that turns and tilts the kettle forward or backward. When you stop turning the handle, the kettle holds its position. Product in the tilting kettles can also be cooked in a basket, and the method of removal is the same as that for a stationary kettle.

Cleaning

Prior to cleaning the steam-jacketed kettle, make sure that the unit is off by turning the thermostat to the OFF position and the power switch to the OFF position. If the unit is to be down for a period of time, shut off the gas supply to the unit and/or the electrical service at the breaker box. The kettle should be cleaned as soon as possible after use while it is still warm. This prevents the food from hardening and makes the cleaning job easier. Keep water and cleaning solutions away from the control console, burners, and the electrical connections. Never spray or hose down the exterior of the kettle.

To clean the kettle:

- Remove food residue that has stuck to it by scraping with a brush, cloth, or sponge. If the sticking persists, soak the interior of the kettle with a solution of detergent and water and heat the kettle briefly. Do not use any metal implements such as a metal scraper, spatula, or steel wool; these scratch the surface and make the unit even harder to clean next time. Surface scratches also provide a place for bacteria to grow.
- Wash the inside of the kettle with a mixture of detergent and hot water.
- Rinse thoroughly with hot water and drain the kettle completely.
- Sanitize the equipment with an approved sanitizing solution according to the manufacturer's directions. Never leave the sanitizing solution in the kettle for longer than 30 minutes as corrosion of the stainless steel could occur.
- After the unit has been cleaned, sanitized, and drained, let all the surfaces air dry.
- When the interior of the kettle is clean, wipe down the exterior surface and the control panel with a damp clean cloth. If desired, the exterior surface may be polished with a stainless steel polish.

In some areas, mineral deposits may be left in the kettle by hard water. If this is the case, after cleaning, use a de-liming agent in accordance with the manufacturer's directions and thoroughly rinse the pan.

Maintenance

Water level—Check the water level daily by looking at the gauge glass (see Figure 6.24). The water level should be between the MAX and MIN levels on the glass. If it is low, add water. Do not use tap water; use distilled or treated water only. (A water treatment compound can be obtained from the manufacturer of your kettle.) Let the kettle cool. To add water:

- Remove the pipe plug from the fill assembly.
- Open the gate valve and pour in the distilled or treated water. While pouring the water, hold the safety valve open to allow air to escape.
- Pour the water until the level rises to a point between the MIN and MAX levels on the water gauge. Any air that gets into the jacket must be removed for the unit to operate correctly.

Jacket vacuum—When the kettle is cold, check the vacuum gauge reading (see Figure 6.25). This should be done on a daily basis. The reading should be between the 20 and 30 below zero mark. A reading near or above zero indicates

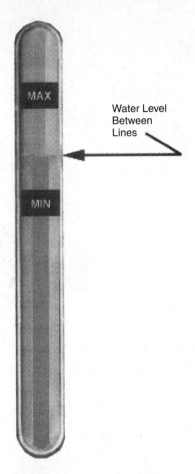

FIGURE 6.24   Water level gauge.

Source: Groen.

that there is air in the jacket and the unit will not heat properly. To remove the air:

- Put water or product into the kettle and turn the kettle on.
- The elbow of the safety valve should be directed toward the floor.
- When the pressure/vacuum gauge reaches 5 PSI, pull up or out on the safety valve lever or ring for one second.
- Repeat this procedure and then let the pull ring or valve lever snap back into the closed position.

Safety valve—Check the safety valve on a daily basis (see Figure 6.26). With 5 PSI pressure in the jacket, lift the safety valve lever for five seconds. Release the lever

FIGURE 6.25   Vacuum gauge.

Source: Cleveland.

FIGURE 6.26 Pressure safety valve.

Source: Groen.

and let the valve snap shut. If the lever does not activate, if there is no steam discharge, or if the valve leaks, shut the unit down immediately and contact an authorized repair technician.

BRAISING PAN

Overview

Braising pans are also known as tilt skillets. They are probably the most versatile piece of equipment in the kitchen because they can braise, fry, sauté, bake, roast, and function as a griddle, fry pan, oven, bain-marie, or food warmer. They are most advantageous when producing large quantities of product and are thus ideally suited for banquet kitchens, institutional foodservice, and large production kitchens. They can be operated by using either gas or electricity (see Figure 6.27).

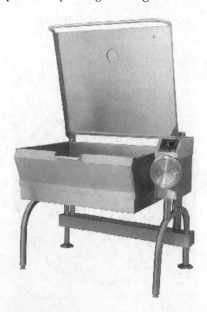

FIGURE 6.27

Source: Cleveland.

Parts

- Power ON switch—Turns the unit on and shuts it off. *Note:* Some manufacturers do not have a power switch. Setting the thermostat to the desired temperature simultaneously turns the unit's power on.
- Thermostat—Controls the cooking temperature. The normal range is between 175°F (80°C) and 425°F (220°C) on gas units and 100°F (38°C) and 400°F (204°C) on electric units.
- Indicator light (electric only)—Indicates when the electric heating element is on.
- Lift device—Either a manually operated worm and gear mechanism controlled by a hand wheel, a tilting handle, or an electrically operated mechanism that raises and lowers the pan (see Figure 6.28).

Operation

- Place the product to be cooked into the braising pan. If the unit is equipped with a power switch, turn it on and adjust the thermostat to the desired temperature. (Consult the recipe for the correct temperature.) If the product is to be braised or fried, preheat the pan at 300°F (149°C) or less for 15 minutes and then place the product in the pan. Do not heat an empty pan for longer than five minutes at a temperature over 300°F (149°C) since it could result in damage to the unit. For simmering, a temperature of 210°F (99°C) or less is recommended.
- Most models come equipped with a cover or lid. Place the cover down to reduce moisture loss unless you are drying a product or reducing stock, in which case the cover should be left up. For partial steam escape, there is a vent on top of the lid that can be left open during the cooking process. Avoid contact with the steam escaping from the vent because it could cause a severe burn.
- To check the product while it is cooking, stand to the side of the pan to avoid being burned by the steam that will be released and slowly lift the cover. On most models, the cover stays in the open position until it is pushed down.
- When the product is finished cooking, transfer it to a storage or service container. Select one that is deep enough to prevent splashing as the product

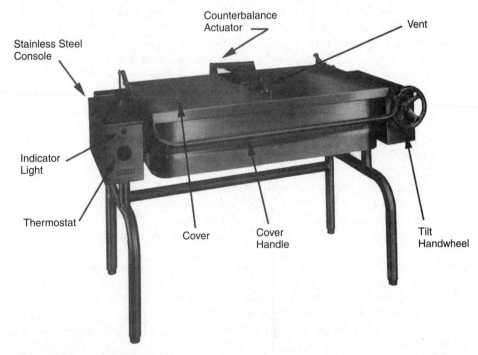

FIGURE 6.28 Braising pan parts.

Source: Groen.

is poured from the pan into the storage container. Make sure that the container is on a flat surface and is stable. To transfer the product:

- If the braising pan is equipped with a power switch, turn it to the OFF position.
- Turn the thermostat to the OFF position.
- Lift the lid of the braising pan.
- Tilt the pan forward by either manually turning the hand wheel, pulling the tilting handle down, or turning on the automatic tilting device.
- When you stop turning the hand wheel, pulling on the tilting handle, or releasing the automatic device, the pan holds the position it is in.
- When the pan is tilted, the gas supply to the pan shuts off.
- While pouring from the braising pan into the container, stand to the side to avoid being splashed by the hot contents. (Items that have been cooked in a liquid, such as a sauce or melted shortening, can slide forward suddenly during the tilting process.)
- When the product has been emptied, return the braising pan to its original flat position.
- Remember to use the proper cooling procedure for large volumes of hot products.

Cleaning

Before cleaning the braising pan:

- Make sure that the unit is turned off by turning the thermostat, as well as (if the unit has one) the power switch, to the OFF position.
- If the unit is to be down for a period of time, shut off the gas supply to the unit and/or the electrical service at the breaker box.
- The pan should be cleaned as soon as possible after use while it is still warm. This prevents the food from hardening and makes the cleaning job easier.
- Keep water and cleaning solutions away from the control console, burners, and the electrical connections.
- Never spray or hose down the exterior of the pan.

To clean the pan:

- Remove food residue that has stuck to the pan by scraping it with a brush, cloth, or sponge. If the sticking persists, soak the pan with a solution of detergent and water and heat the pan briefly. Do not use any metal implements such as a metal scraper, spatula, or steel wool since these will scratch the surface which will make the pan even harder to clean and will also provide a place for bacteria to grow.
- Wash the inside of the pan with a mixture of detergent and hot water, mixed according to the manufacturer's directions. Wipe down the underside of the pan cover. Rinse everything thoroughly with hot water and drain the pan completely.
- Sanitize the equipment with a solution of 200 parts per million available chlorine or an approved sanitizing solution and rinse thoroughly. Never leave the sanitizing solution in the pan for longer than 30 minutes as corrosion of the stainless steel could occur.
- After the unit has been cleaned, sanitized, and drained, let all the surfaces air dry.
- When the interior of the pan is clean, wipe down the exterior surface and the control panel with a damp clean cloth. If desired, the exterior surface may be polished with a stainless steel polish. In some areas, mineral deposits may be left in the pan by hard water. If this is the case, after cleaning, use a de-liming agent in accordance with the manufacturer's directions and thoroughly rinse the pan.

Maintenance

Twice a year, the trunnion bearings should be greased. With gas units, it may be necessary to adjust the pilot light and burners from time to time.

Authorized service personnel should check the unit once a year.

HOODS, MAKEUP AIR, AND FIRE SUPPRESSANT SYSTEMS

Overview

When you stand in the kitchen and look at the hood over the cook's line, it looks like a simple system. Hot greasy air gets sucked into the hood and blown out somewhere on the roof. In reality, it is not a single system, but rather several complex systems all coming together in the hood. There is the hood itself, the duct system, the exhaust fan, the **makeup air system**, and the fire suppressant system. All these are governed by various codes and the codes change from jurisdiction to jurisdiction (see Figure 6.29).

FIGURE 6.29
Source: Captiveaire.

Hoods

Hoods are constructed of either stainless steel or galvanized steel. Most jurisdictional law requires them over each and every piece of cooking equipment in the kitchen. Other than the law, there are three reasons to have a hood in the kitchen: They (1) remove heat and grease, (2) improve air circulation throughout the kitchen thus increasing employee comfort, and (3) prevent cooking equipment fires from spreading.

To prevent fires, the size as well as the placement of the hood is critical. These are governed by the National Fire Protection Association (NFPA) Code and are as follows:

- The minimum height of the hood itself should be 2 feet.
- The distance from the top of the equipment to the base of the hood should not exceed 4 feet.
- The distance from the floor to the base of the hood should be between 6 feet 6 inches and 7 feet.
- There should be 2 inches of hood overhang for every foot between the top of the equipment to the base of the hood. Therefore, if the distance between the top of the equipment and the base of the hood is the maximum of 4 feet, the hood would overhang the equipment 8 inches (see Figure 6.30).

An exhaust fan on the roof removes the hot and greasy air from the kitchen. It pulls the air from beneath the hood through the duct(s) and to the outside at a rate of 1,500 cubic feet per minute (CFM). The size of the hood, size of the kitchen, length and number of bends in the ductwork, and several other variables are calculated to determine the number of horsepower necessary in the fan to achieve the air removal at 1,500 CFM.

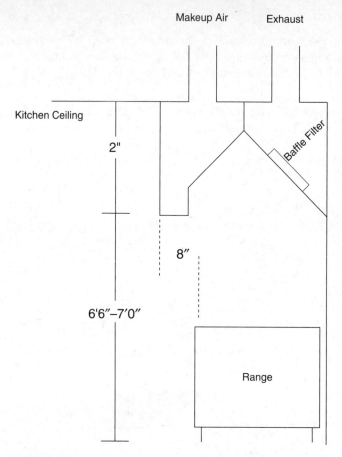

FIGURE 6.30 A diagram showing the hood dimensions, height, and overhang.

As the air leaves the hood and prior to going through the ductwork, it passes through baffle filters. The purpose of the filters is to remove most of the grease in the air so that it does not pollute the outside atmosphere. Some exhaust systems employ a series of extractor modules rather than filters to achieve this purpose. Some hoods also come equipped with a self-cleaning module that washes the ducts and hood to keep them free from grease buildup. The latest self-cleaning concept on the market is the placement of an ultraviolet light system in the hood. The light disintegrates the grease, keeping the entire system clean (see Figure 6.31).

MAKEUP AIR With air leaving the building at the rate of 1,500 CFM, it needs to be replaced. Most jurisdictions require that the exhausted air be made up of fresh air at the rate of 80 percent. The other 20 percent comes from the dining room, hallways, doors, windows, etc. To replenish the exhausted air, a makeup air system is used. This entails an intake air vent with a rain hood on the roof of the building, a fan to bring the air in, a heating/cooling device to temper the outside air, and a discharge vent in the hood.

There are basically three different types of discharge vents: winter, summer, and short cycle.

1. The winter vent is located on the front of the hood at the top (see Figure 6.32). The makeup air is pushed out of the vent, circulates throughout the kitchen, and is eventually pulled into the hood and exhausted out of the roof discharge.
2. With the summer discharge, also known as a curtain discharge, the vent is located at the bottom of the front of the hood and blows the air directly down, forming an air curtain between the equipment on the cook's line and

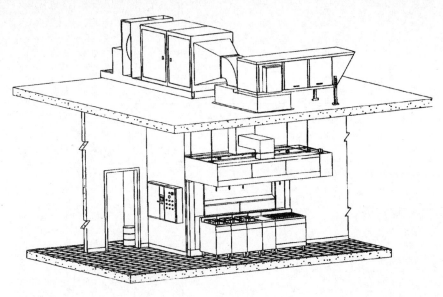

FIGURE 6.31 A diagram showing the kitchen exhaust going up to the roof and the makeup air return.

the kitchen (see Figure 6.33). Some hoods are equipped with the winter discharge system only, some have summer discharge only, and some have both. Some also have a variation of either.

3. With both the summer and/or winter discharge systems, the air coming into the kitchen from the outside is tempered; that is, it is either heated or cooled depending on the season of the year. For example, in the middle of the summer

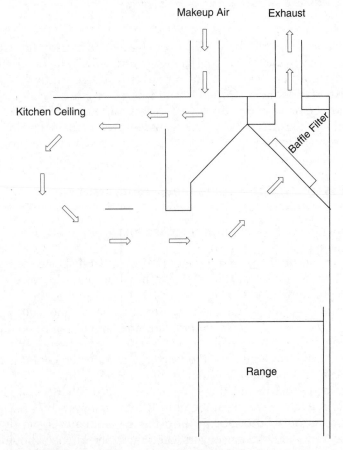

FIGURE 6.32 Winter makeup air system.

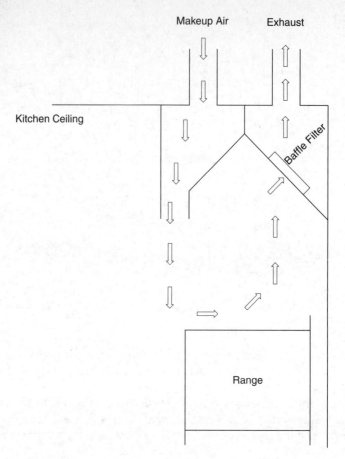

FIGURE 6.33 Summer makeup air system.

you wouldn't want 90°F (32°C) air coming into an already hot kitchen; conversely, in the winter, you wouldn't want 20°F (–7°C) air chilling the kitchen.

4. With the short cycle system, the air never really gets into the kitchen (see Figure 6.34). It comes through a vent located on the back side of the front panel of the hood and is directed by an air diffuser through the filters and out through the duct to the roof. Because air never enters the kitchen, it does not need to be tempered. *Note:* Some jurisdictions will not approve the short cycle makeup air system.

FIRE SUPPRESSANT SYSTEMS   All **fire suppressant systems** have similarities (see Figure 6.35).

• They all put out fires by smothering the source of the fire, thus depriving it of oxygen.
• They all have nozzles coming out of the hood that disperse the fire suppressant material. These nozzles, by law, must be placed over each piece of cooking equipment in the kitchen. The distance between the nozzle and the equipment, as well as the temperature at which the nozzle discharges its material, is determined by the type and makeup of the particular piece of equipment.
• When the system activates, the power source to the cooking equipment (electricity, gas, or both) is automatically shut off.
• Should a fire occur and the system does not discharge automatically, a manual activator switch can be used to start the system (see Figure 6.36). This, by law, must be located by the exit that would most logically be used in the event of a fire. All employees working in the kitchen should know the location of this switch and how to activate it.

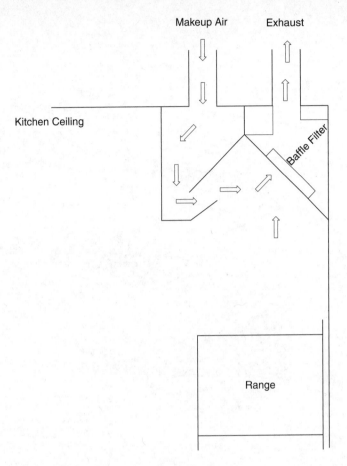

FIGURE 6.34   Short cycle makeup air system.

While all fire suppressant systems operate similarly, there are four different materials that are used to actually put the fire out. They are powder, foam, water mist, and a combination of water mist and foam.

- The powder system is no longer manufactured; however, many kitchens still have this material. When the system discharges, a very fine powder is blown out of the nozzle and down over the equipment where it smothers the fire. While most of it blows down, some of it blows out over the kitchen and gets into everything. Months after the system is activated and the kitchen cleaned and reopened, powder is still found.
- Foam is the material found in most systems. When the fire suppressant system is activated, foam is discharged from the nozzles directly onto the equipment. It, like the powder, smothers the fire. It, like the powder, goes everywhere.

The bad news is that it takes a day or more to clean up the powder or foam. The good news is the building didn't burn down.

Both the powder and foam systems are activated by a fusible link located in the hood behind the filters (see Figure 6.37). (When the filters are removed for cleaning, you can actually see the links in the hood.) The powder or foam is stored under pressure in a tank. When a fire occurs, the heat from the fire melts the link and activates the system. The powder or foam travels under pressure from the tank, through a pipe to the nozzles, and blows out of the nozzles under the hood and onto the equipment, smothering the fire. As mentioned earlier, the equipment power source is simultaneously turned off.

When the tank empties, the powder or foam is gone. This is one of the drawbacks of these systems in that the fire may not be extinguished when the

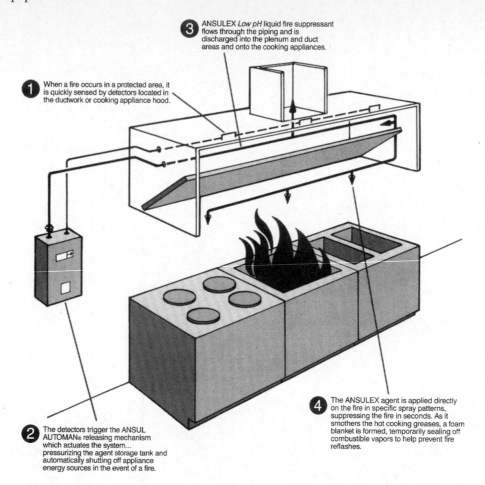

③ ANSULEX *Low pH* liquid fire suppressant flows through the piping and is discharged into the plenum and duct areas and onto the cooking appliances.

① When a fire occurs in a protected area, it is quickly sensed by detectors located in the ductwork or cooking appliance hood.

④ The ANSULEX agent is applied directly on the fire in specific spray patterns, suppressing the fire in seconds. As it smothers the hot cooking greases, a foam blanket is formed, temporarily sealing off combustible vapors to help prevent fire reflashes.

② The detectors trigger the ANSUL AUTOMAN® releasing mechanism which actuates the system... pressurizing the agent storage tank and automatically shutting off appliance energy sources in the event of a fire.

FIGURE 6.35 Fire suppressant system using a liquid that turns to foam upon impact.

Source: Ansul.

material is used up. Additionally, the fire could re-flash with no material to extinguish it.

- Water mist operates a little differently from the others. It is activated by a glycerin capsule located directly above the nozzle. Heat from the fire melts the capsule and activates the system. A fine mist of water covers the piece of equipment that is on fire and smothers it. An advantage of this system is

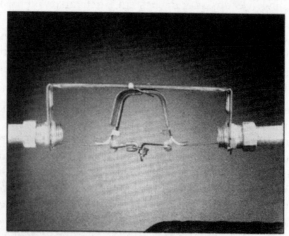

FIGURE 6.36 The fusible link on a fire suppressant system.

Source: Ansul.

FIGURE 6.37 The manual switch on a fire suppressant system.

Source: Ansul.

that only the activated nozzle, directly over the fire, goes off. (Unlike the powder or foam system that activates all the nozzles under the hood.) Should the fire spread, the next capsule melts and activates that nozzle. Another advantage of this system is that it is hooked up to the water line in the building; thus, there is no shortage of fire suppressant material. A possible disadvantage is that there is no manual activation for this system. It should be noted that not all jurisdictions have approved the water mist system.

- The fourth system, a combination of the water mist system and a chemical fire suppressant, is in the development stage. The suppressants being tested are a foam and a gel. After testing, the system will be proposed to the various codes commissions for approval.

Parts

HOOD AND EXHAUST SYSTEM

- Control panel—Contains the ON/OFF switch for the exhaust and makeup air. Sometimes these are the same switch and sometimes they are separate switches. Also contains the switch for the lights under the hood.
- **Baffle filter**—A device that collects most of the grease from the exhausted air. Normally there are several filters in one hood. *Note:* Some hoods operate without filters, using an extractor module within the hood system to extract grease.
- Drip cup—A vessel that collects the grease extracted from the filters or the baffle system.
- Exhaust fan—Located on the roof, the fan pulls out air, in most cases at 1,500 CFM.

MAKEUP AIR

- Air intake vent—A metal duct with a rain hood that directs fresh outside air into the system.
- Filters—Filters the outside air to eliminate dirt, dust, bugs, etc. from entering the system.
- Tempering unit—Heats or cools the outside air being brought in depending on the season. Short cycle systems do not have a tempering unit.
- Hood vents—Direct the makeup air, either out of the front of the hood into the entire kitchen or straight down as an air curtain. Short cycle vents keep the air within the hood and direct it to the exhaust.

FIRE SUPPRESSANT SYSTEM

- Fusible link—A metal piece that melts under the high temperature of a fire and activates the system. Water mist systems use a glycerin capsule for the same purpose.
- Holding tank—Contains the fire suppressant material, either powder or foam. Water mist systems do not have a holding tank but are hooked up to the building waterline.
- Manual switch—Activates the fire suppressant system manually. Located at the most logical exit to the kitchen should a fire occur. Water mist systems do not have a manual activation switch.

Operation

Prior to starting any cooking equipment, start the exhaust system by turning the ON/OFF switch to the ON position. This, in most cases, turns on both the exhaust and makeup air. If they are separate switches, turn them both on at this time. *Note:* Cooking equipment should not be turned on until the exhaust system is turned on and is functioning. Turn the hood lights on at this time.

In the event of a fire, the fire suppressant system should activate automatically. Should it fail, use the manual switch to activate it as you are exiting the kitchen. Make sure that all employees know the location of the switch and how to use it. Prior to leaving the kitchen, make sure that everyone is out. Keep everyone, including yourself, calm during the evacuation. *Note:* There is no manual switch for the water mist system.

Cleaning

Daily:

- Clean the interior and exterior of the hood with a clean cloth rinsed in a mild detergent solution.
- Remove the grease cup and empty it in the grease barrel.
- Clean the cup and replace it.
- If the exterior of the hood is stainless steel, it can be polished with a stainless steel polish.

Weekly:

- Remove the filters or the cartridges. They can be cleaned in either the pot and pan sink or the dish machine.
- Check and clean the interior surfaces behind the filters.
- Dry and replace the filters.

Maintenance

Semiannually:

- Have the hood and ductwork cleaned by a professional duct cleaning company. Check with your local authorities, since some codes require that this be done more often.
- Have the fire suppressant system checked by the company that installed it or by an authorized fire suppressant company.

Note: The fire department often inspects the hoods, ducts, and fire suppressant systems in commercial foodservice operations. They also inspect the premises for the proper placement of fire extinguishers as well as the tags showing when they were recharged.

Questions

1. Discuss the sources of steam used to operate steam equipment.
2. What is the difference between a convection oven and a conventional oven? Describe the application of each.
3. Explain the different styles of steam kettles and what each would be used for.
4. What is the most versatile piece of cooking equipment in the kitchen? Give its applications of use.
5. Explain how a microwave oven works.
6. What is the purpose of a hood in the kitchen?
7. What are the three types of makeup air? Which type(s) need their air tempered?
8. Tell how each of the three fire suppressant systems work.

Project

Conduct a training session of the steam equipment in your school lab kitchen for all new students.

Acknowledgments

Amana Commercial and Industrial Products Division, Amana IA.
AVTEC Industries Inc., Oswego, IL.
Blodgett Corporation, Burlington, VT.
Garland Commercial, Freeland, PA.

Gemini Corporation, Philadelphia, PA.
GROEN, Jackson, MS.
Middleby-Marshall, Elgin, IL.
Vulcan-Hart, Louisville, KY.

Web Sites

Amana Commercial and Industrial Products Division
www.amanacommercial.com

AVTEC Industries Inc.
www.avtecind.com

Blodgett Corporation
www.maytagfoodservice.com

Bunn-O-Matic Corporation
www.bunn.com

Cres-Cor
www.crescor.com

Garland Commercial Ind.
www.garland-group.com

GROEN
www.groen.com

Middleby Marshall
www.middleby.com

Keating of Chicago
www.keatingofchicago.com

Vulcan-Hart
www.vulcanhart.com

Wolf Range Co.
www.wolfrange.com

Resources

Birchfield, John C. (1998). Design and Layout of Foodservice Facilities. New York, NY: John Wiley & Sons, Inc.
Katsigris, Costas & Thomas, Chris (1999). Design and Equipment for Restaurants and Foodservice: A Management View. New York, NY: John Wiley & Sons, Inc.
Kazarian, Edward A. (1997). Foodservice Facilities Planning, 3rd ed. New York, NY: John Wiley & Sons, Inc.
Scriven, C. & Stevens, J. (1982). Food Equipment Facts. New York, NY: John Wiley & Sons, Inc.

Product specification sheets and owners manual from the following companies:

Ansul Fire Protection
Amana Commercial & Industrial Products Division

AVTEC Industries Inc.
Blodgett Corporation
Garland Commercial Industries
Gemini Corp
GROEN Co.
The Middleby Marshall Corp.
Rational Cooking Systems Inc.
Vulcan-Hart

CHAPTER 7

Refrigeration

Objectives

Upon completion of this chapter, you will be able to:

- Identify the key components of a refrigeration system and tell how the system works.
- Calibrate a thermometer.
- Demonstrate the cleaning and maintenance of a reach-in and walk-in cooler.
- Explain the operation of an ice machine and define the term "ice machine capacity."
- Tell the difference between a premix fountain beverage dispenser and a postmix dispenser.

Key Terms

air-cooled systems
compressor
condenser
evaporator
ice harvest
premix

postmix
R-22
thermometer
thermostat
water-cooled systems

INTRODUCTION

Is heat the absence of cold or is cold the absence of heat? In the case of refrigeration, clearly, cold is the absence of heat; that is, for something to become refrigerated or frozen, heat must be removed. To do this, refrigeration systems rely on latent heat, which is the amount of heat necessary to change a liquid into a gas. This is also known as vaporization. For example, if a pan of water is put on a stove and the stove is turned on, eventually the water boils, or, to put it another way, the liquid (water) turns into a gas (vapor). The water pulls heat particles from the heat source and keeps on pulling these heat particles until it changes from liquid into gas.

How does all of this discussion about heat relate to keeping something cold? Simple. Refrigeration systems use a CFC-free refrigerant called **R-22**, which boils at –32°F (–36°C). R-22 goes throughout the refrigeration system as a liquid. As it goes, it pulls out heat particles from the products in the refrigerator or freezer. It keeps on pulling these heat particles until it boils and turns into a gas at –32°F (–36°C).

The R-22 refrigerant is very expensive. Because of this, we don't want it to evaporate when it turns into a gas. We also don't want our refrigerators and the products in them to be at –32°F (–36°C) all of the time; therefore, we need additional parts to operate a refrigeration system. To look at it in its most basic format, we need a compressor, condenser, evaporator, and thermostat. There are other components, but comprehending these and how they work gives you a basic understanding of how a refrigeration system operates (see Figure 7.1).

- The **compressor**—The refrigerant R-22, which is in a gaseous state, is compressed until it gets very hot.
- The **condenser**—Takes the hot R-22 gas and condenses it into a liquid form.

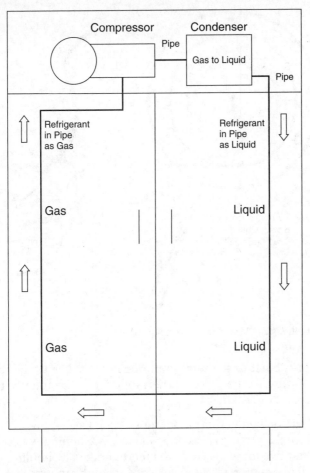

FIGURE 7.1 Refrigeration cycle showing the refrigerant as a liquid leaving the condenser, changing to a gas as it picks up heat particles from the interior of the refrigerator, and returning it to the compressor as a gas (vapor).

- The **evaporator**—Takes the R-22, now in a liquid state and circulates it. As it circulates throughout the refrigerator or freezer, it picks up heat particles from the air in the box as well as from the product. As it picks up these heat particles, it heats up until it comes to the boiling point and turns into a gas. It returns to the compressor, where the process starts over and repeats itself.
- The **thermostat**—Controls the temperature in the box. There are normally two temperatures on the thermostat, a low setting and a high setting. When the temperature in the box reaches the high setting, the refrigeration system is turned on. The liquid refrigerant:

> Circulates throughout the evaporator (the box) picking up heat particles.
> Comes to a boil and turns into a gas.
> Returns to the compressor and gets compressed.
> Goes to the condenser and gets condensed into a liquid.
> Goes on to the evaporator as a liquid.
> This continues until the temperature in the box reaches the low setting on the thermostat.

When this happens, the thermostat shuts the system down. Example: If you wanted the temperature in your refrigerator to be 35°F (2°C), you could set the parameters on your thermostat at 37°F (3°C) and 33°F (1°C), when the temperature in the box reaches 37°F (3°C), the system goes on. When it reaches 33°F (1°C), the system goes off.

- **Thermometer**—Most commercial units contain exterior thermometers on their refrigerators and freezers. These work by use of a probe that is in the

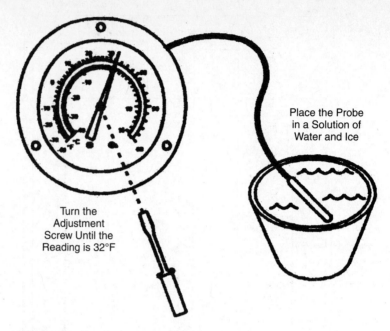

Place the Probe
in a Solution of
Water and Ice

Turn the
Adjustment
Screw Until the
Reading is 32°F

FIGURE 7.2 Thermometer recalibration.

interior cabinet of the refrigerator or freezer. The probe relays the interior temperature to the exterior thermometer. Occasionally these need to be recalibrated. To do this:

Remove the interior probe from its clip (see Figure 7.2).
Place the probe in a solution of slush containing water and ice.
After five minutes, check the thermometer. It should read 32°F (0°C).
If it does not, remove the plastic face of the thermometer.
Holding the thermometer pointer in place, turn the adjustment screw with a screwdriver clockwise to lower the temperature reading or counterclockwise to increase the reading.
Let go of the pointer. If the reading is not 32°F (0°C), repeat the previous step until it reaches 32°F (0°C).
Replace the plastic cover and place the probe back in its clip.

Some health departments accept the temperature reading of an exterior thermometer, although most will not. For safety, in addition to the exterior thermometer, it is recommended that a thermometer be hung on the center of the interior of the refrigerator or freezer.

One more thing: The condenser gives off considerable heat. This heat has to go somewhere and it can go either into water or into the air surrounding the refrigeration system. Thus, we have two types of refrigeration systems: water-cooled and air-cooled. **Water-cooled systems** have a series of pipes containing water. The water picks up the heat particles given off by the condenser and becomes quite hot. In "state-of-the-art" facilities, where having a "green kitchen" is important, this water is circulated into the hot water system. By doing this, the hot water heater does not have to work as hard to get the water up to the desired temperature and therefore uses less energy. In operations that do not do this, the hot water is simply emptied into a floor drain.

Air-cooled systems are the most popular and are therefore found in most commercial refrigerators and freezers. In this system, a fan blows the hot air off the condenser into the surrounding air in the room. It is critical that, for this system to operate most efficiently, the fins on the condenser be cleaned on a regular basis, preferably monthly.

Freezers work in the same way as refrigeration systems except that they use a different refrigerant called R-404.

REACH-IN REFRIGERATORS AND FREEZERS

Overview

While discussing reach-in refrigerators and freezers, other refrigeration units are also included (see Figure 7.3). Refrigerated display cases, salad/sandwich makeup units, pizza tables, and refrigerated drawers on the cook's line all have basically the same characteristics as reach-ins, except that they are not as well insulated (see Figures 7.4 and 7.5). Because of this, they are not used for long-term storage like a reach-in.

Display cases are meant to impulse-sell product to the customer. Being in the front of the house, they also make it easier for service personnel to obtain salads or refrigerated desserts where they need them, close to the guests.

Makeup units, pizza tables, and refrigerated drawers make it easier for the line cooks to produce meals without running to a reach-in to obtain product. They are designed to get the operation through the rush period. Having goods at one's fingertips saves time and unnecessary traffic. At the end of the shift or at closing time, product stored in these units should be returned to either a reach-in or walk-in refrigerator. The cleaning and maintenance procedures on these units are identical to reach-ins.

Operation

Only two components need to be adjusted on a reach-in refrigerator or freezer and usually only at the time of delivery. After that they are probably set for life. They are the thermostat on the refrigerator and/or freezer and the defrost cycle on the freezer. While both of these are set at the factory, your particular requirements may require a different setting. For example, if the reach-in refrigerator is located on the line and is used to store fresh fish, it would be set at 33°F (1°C). If it is located in the garde-manger kitchen and is used for fresh produce, you would probably want it set at 38°F (3°C).

The thermostat is normally located on the top of the unit. Some thermostats come with the actual degrees listed on the dial, but most use a series of

FIGURE 7.3 Two-door, reach-in refrigerator.
Source: Delfield.

FIGURE 7.4 Refrigerated display case.
Source: Delfield.

numbers ranging from 1 upwards. If the numbers range from 1 to 8, 4 is average and would give the temperature desired in most cases. Be careful, because on most models, the higher the number, the lower the temperature. Thus 1 would be the warmest the box would get, and 8 would be the coldest. Check the

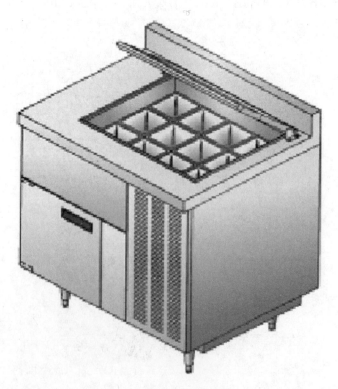

FIGURE 7.5 Refrigerated sandwich makeup unit. Also known as a salad makeup unit or a refrigerated pizza table.
Source: Delfield.

manufacturer's literature to make sure that this is the sequence being used in your particular model.

The defrost cycle is set at the factory, and most manufacturers set it so that it will defrost every six hours, or four times a day. Should you not want this sequence, the setting can be changed. At the top of the freezer, behind the front panel, is a 24-hour clock that indicates when the defrost cycle will occur. Move the pointer to control the number of defrost cycles during a 24-hour period, as well as the time at which you want the defrost function to occur.

Cleaning

During the cleaning process, the shelving should be disassembled. While a few models have permanent shelving, the vast majority are equipped with removable shelving. There are basically two types of removable shelving: clips and glides.

With clip shelving, there are four posts inside the reach-in. One is located at the front left-hand side of the reach-in, one at the front right, one at the back left, and one at the back right. Slots in the posts allow a clip to be inserted. Four clips are inserted in the four posts and the shelf rests on these clips. By moving the clips, you can make different shelving configurations. For example, there could be 12 inches between two shelves and 6 inches between two other shelves. In this way, the reach-in can be utilized to its maximum potential.

Glide shelving has two sets of glides installed in the interior of the reach-in, one each on the left-hand and right-hand side. The shelving slides in place on these glides. Like the clip style, many different configurations of shelving can be made.

The interiors of reach-in refrigerators and freezers can be cleaned using a nonabrasive detergent and water mixed according to the manufacturer's recommendations. If a spill or soil is particularly tough, ammonia and water can be used, again mixed according to the manufacturer's recommendations. Use a cloth or soft sponge to clean the unit.

The exterior of the unit can also be cleaned with a nonabrasive detergent and water. If the exterior is made of stainless steel, a stainless cleaner and polish can be applied with a clean cloth. Never use a metal sponge or any other abrasive substance, such as an SOS or Chore Girl pad, to clean either the interior or exterior surface.

Refrigerators should be emptied and cleaned at least weekly and freezers monthly. Should a spill occur, the unit should be cleaned immediately.

Maintenance

One of the most important and most often overlooked maintenance duties in the kitchen is the cleaning of the condenser fins. This should be done monthly or more often if the fins are completely blocked when the unit is cleaned. To clean the fins, use a vacuum cleaner or a stiff brush to remove the dust, dirt, and grease.

Another maintenance procedure is the inspection of the door gaskets. This should be done when the unit is deep cleaned. If the gaskets are cracked or worn, they should be replaced. The purpose of the gaskets is to ensure a complete seal around the door, trapping the cold air in and keeping the warm air of the kitchen out of the refrigerator or freezer. A cracked or worn gasket allows moisture into the unit and forces the unit to work overtime, drastically shortening the life of the refrigeration component.

WALK-IN COOLERS AND FREEZERS

Overview

Walk-in coolers and freezers are designed for long-term storage, while reach-in coolers and freezers are intended for short-term storage or frequently used products. Because of their size, walk-ins take longer to recover to their proper temperature

FIGURE 7.6
Source: Kolpak.

level than reach-ins when the door is opened. Hence, the less a walk-in is entered, the better. The products stay at their intended temperature and less energy is expended. Plastic strips or air curtains can be used to reduce the cold air escaping when the walk-in door is opened (see Figure 7.6). There are three different methods of construction for walk-in coolers and freezers.

The first type is a walk-in that is actually built as part of the building, similar to a room. This method is normally reserved for extremely large walk-ins that are found in a large food distribution warehouse, a central commissary, or a large institutional kitchen.

The second type, used for small walk-ins, is completely built in the factory as an integral unit. It is transported from the factory on a flat bed truck to the foodservice operation. Normally this type is used as an outdoor unit as opposed to a unit in the kitchen, as it is too large to fit through a standard door frame.

The third type, which is the most popular and is used for small- and medium-sized walk-ins, is a modularly constructed unit (see Figure 7.7). For most manufacturers, the wall modules are 8-feet high, 4-inches thick, and are 1–3 feet in width. These modules are hooked together on site. The floor and ceiling of the walk-in are assembled in a similar manner. The door module contains the interior light, light switch, and the thermometer, thus all of the electrical components are located on this section. Consequently, any size walk-in can be constructed without having to worry about getting it through a door or ripping out an exterior wall to get the walk-in into the kitchen.

Parts

- Door—Can be left opening, right opening, or sliding. All walk-in doors must be fitted with an inside release on the door latch to prevent a person from being trapped inside. This release must function whether or not the door is padlocked.
- Door gasket—A rubber strip that goes around the door to ensure a tight fit when the door is closed.

FIGURE 7.7 A modular walk-in refrigerator/freezer. The panels are joined together with a cam locking device.

Source: Kolpak.

- Door heating strip—A wire that goes around the perimeter interior of the door to slightly heat the door edge, thus preventing excessive condensation from forming. This strip is particularly important in freezers since the condensation could freeze the door shut. In many walk-ins, the strip is located in the door gasket.
- Door panel (see Figure 7.8)—On most small- to medium-sized walk-ins, several additional components are located on the door panel, including:
  ○ The interior light switch.
  ○ Interior light enclosed in a vapor-proof glass.
  ○ Thermometer.
  ○ Pressure relief vent, needed to avoid a vacuum from being created by different temperatures and air pressures when the door is closed.
- Defrost time clock—Controls the frequency of the defrost cycles. While factory set, it may need to be adjusted depending on the temperature and humidity of the room in which the walk-in is located. The amount of time that the walk-in door is open and the type of product being stored also affect the number of defrost cycles.

1	Door Closure
2	Vapor Proof Light (Interior)
3	Dial Thermometer
4	Light Switch/Pilot Light
5	Latch and Safety Release
6	Foot Treadle (Optional)
7	Heater Cable
8	Reinforced Door Sill
9	Cam Lift Hinge

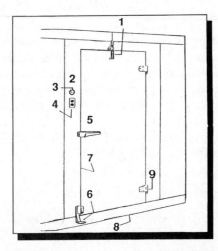

FIGURE 7.8 Parts of a walk-in door panel.

Source: Kolpak.

Operation

- Store frozen foods at 0°F (–18°C) or below. Refrigerated foods should be stored at 33°F (–41°C) depending on the product. For example, fish and poultry at 33° C and produce at 41° C.
- Items that need to be the coldest, such as poultry and fish, should be stored at the back of the walk-in on a lower shelf.
- Store all items on the shelves and off the floor.
- Do not overcrowd the walk-in because air circulation is important to maintain a constant temperature.
- When removing product, use the FIFO (first-in-first-out) method to assure that the oldest product gets used first.
- Do not store cooked product and raw product together in the same container. Cooked product should be stored above raw product.
- Everything in the walk-in should be either wrapped or placed in an airtight container and marked according to contents and dated.

Cleaning

- Wipe up any spills immediately.
- Monthly, or more frequently if needed, wipe down the interior and exterior walls, ceiling, floor, and shelving with a clean cloth that has been saturated and wrung dry in a solution of water and mild detergent.
- For heavy stains, a mild nonabrasive cleanser can be used.
- If the exterior is stainless steel, a thin coat of stainless steel polish can be applied according to the manufacturer's directions.
- Do not wet mop or wash the walk-in with a hose, because excess water damages the panels and could seep inside the panel and destroy the insulation. In most cases, the manufacturer's warranty will be voided if this occurs.
- Also monthly, clean the door gaskets using a solution of baking soda and warm water to wash them. Wipe the gaskets dry with a clean cloth.

Maintenance

As needed.

Should there be a frequent frost buildup on the evaporator, increase the number of defrost cycles per day in the defrost time clock.

MONTHLY

- Inspect door gaskets for wear. Make sure that the gasket is properly seated inside its retainer. Replace gaskets as needed.
- Check the heater wire around the door opening. It should be warm to the touch. Also check for frost or sweating. If this occurs, call a qualified service contractor to replace the heater wire.
- Check the interior of the walk-in for missing plug buttons and replace them if they are missing. This prevents moisture from getting into the insulation inside the wall panel.

QUARTERLY

- Lubricate the door hinges with petroleum jelly (see Figure 7.9). Check the hinge screws and tighten them if necessary.
- Clean the condenser coils with a vacuum, being careful not to bend the fins.

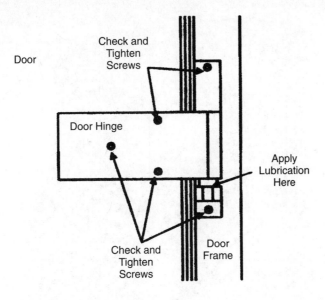

Typical Door Hinge

FIGURE 7.9 Typical door hinge.

Source: Kolpak.

ICE MACHINE, ICE STORAGE BIN, AND DISPENSER

Overview

While ice machines and ice storage bins look like one piece of equipment, for the most part, they are separate elements—often purchased and shipped separately. For example, you could purchase an ice machine with a 750-pound production capacity and place it on a bin. If you need more capacity, another 750-pound machine could be stacked on top of your present machine, doubling the ice output. Most manufacturers can stack up to three machines. The only caveat is that the storage bin should be large enough to handle the output of the two or three machines.

In this section, we will treat ice machines and bins as one component. While they may have been purchased separately, they operate as an integral unit (see Figure 7.10).

The capacity for an ice machine is predicated on a 24-hour day, 60°F (16°C) water temperature, and 70°F (21°C) room temperature. For every 10-degree difference in either the water or room temperature, there is a 10 percent variance in the ice production. Thus, if the 750-pound ice machine were placed in the middle of the kitchen with an average temperature of 90°F (32°C), it would produce only 600 pounds of ice in a 24-hour period (750 pounds less 20 percent of capacity, or 150 pounds). While average ice consumption per customer varies with the type of service offered and climatic conditions, a rule of thumb for restaurants is a half a pound of ice per customer per day.

While there are minor differences in the method of making ice, the majority of manufacturers use the same process:

- A prechilled evaporator contains cube cells. An even level of water flows across the evaporator and into each cube cell, where it freezes.
- The water continues to flow until a complete cube of ice has formed in the cube cell. Having water flow continuously across the evaporator results in a clear cube of ice as opposed to simply filling the cube cell once, which would result in a cloudy cube of ice. With a continuous flow, the impurities in the water do not settle in the cube cell. An ice thickness probe determines when the cube cell is filled and an ice cube has formed. The water flow is then shut off.

FIGURE 7.10
Source: Manitowoc.

- At this point, a hot gas is sent into the evaporator, warming it and causing the ice cubes to slide off the evaporator sheet.
- The cubes slide into a curtain that opens the bin and the cubes slide into the ice storage bin.
- After the cubes pass the curtain, the curtain closes and the process repeats itself. These last three steps are known as the **ice harvest**.
- After a number of harvests, the ice storage bin gets full. The ice being harvested has nowhere to go and consequently it holds the curtain open. When this happens, the ice machine stops functioning.
- At some point, when ice is removed from the bin, the ice that is "hung up" and is holding the curtain open slides down into the storage bin, thus closing the curtain. The ice machine starts up again and the process is repeated.

Note: Instead of a curtain, some machines have a probe in the ice storage bin. When the bin fills, ice touches the probe, which in turn shuts the ice production down until some of the ice is removed from the bin.

Some ice machines, rather than having cube cells, form the ice on a sheet. When the proper thickness of ice forms on this sheet, a hot wire grid comes down on the sheet, cutting the ice into cubes. Flaked ice is made in this fashion with the thickness of the sheet being much less than for cubes. Rather than having a hot wire grid, the thin sheet is broken into flakes.

In addition to cubes, ice can also be formed into halfcubes, minicubes, moons, halfmoons, circles, and several other sizes and shapes. It can also be manufactured as flakes or crushed.

FIGURE 7.11 Ice dispenser.

Source: Manitowoc.

The ice is transported from the ice bin to the area of use, such as a wait station or bar, where it is put into an ice-service bin. If customers are dispensing their own ice at a beverage service station the ice can be put into a dispenser (see Figure 7.11). In high volume operations such as a large cafeteria or fast-food restaurant where the patrons get their own ice and drink, the ice machine is located on top of the dispensing bin, thus eliminating having an employee constantly fill the dispensing bin.

Parts

Switch—Turns the machine on or off.

Wash switch—Starts the wash cycle (on some machines called the clean cycle). On some models the ON/OFF/CLEAN switch are one and the same.

Evaporator—The plate on which the water freezes to form ice.

Operation

There is very little to know regarding the operation of an ice machine, ice storage bin, or service bin. Some health departments require that a scoop be stored inside the bin in an ice scoop holder, while others require that it be stored on the outside of the bin. Still others require that it be stored outside the bin in a sanitizing solution. Check with your local health department regarding the code in your area.

The most important thing to remember is to always use a scoop to retrieve ice. Never ever fill a glass with ice by "running" the glass through the ice storage bin. When the glass breaks (and sooner or later it will), the entire bin must be emptied of ice, cleared of all broken glass particles, wiped down, flushed with clean water, cleaned, sanitized, and refilled with new ice. All this takes time and during this period, you are virtually shut down.

Never store wine, soda, or mixer bottles or fruit in the ice service bin.

Cleaning

The exterior of the ice machine and storage bin should be cleaned on a regular basis as needed. Use a damp clean towel for routine cleaning. For heavier soil, use a nonabrasive cleaner according to the manufacturer's directions. The machine and bin should be cleaned at least every six months and more often than that if the water conditions require it.

ICE MACHINE   When cleaning the interior of the ice machine, there are two functions to complete. One is the cleaning procedure that removes lime and other mineral deposits. The other is the sanitizing procedure, which removes algae and slime. Both should be done separately.

Note: Do not mix cleaner solutions and sanitizing solutions in order to do both procedures at the same time.

- When the machine has completed a harvest cycle, turn it off. If more than one machine feeds a bin, turn all machines off.
- Empty all ice from the ice storage bin.
- Turn the switch to the WASH or CLEAN position.
- Use rubber gloves, an apron, and eye protection when working with the cleaning and sanitizing solutions.
- Adding the cleaning solution to the machine requires that you read the manufacturer's directions. Some manufacturers specify that it be added to the water trough, while others specify that it be added to water level control tube or the control stream box. Use only the cleaning solution that came with the machine. Replacement cleaning solution can be ordered directly from the manufacturer. Failure to correctly use the recommended solution in the proper amount could void the warranty.
- After the cleaning solution has been added, the machine goes through a self-cleaning process. This lasts approximately half an hour.
- Rinse the machine according to the manufacturer's directions.
- Repeat this procedure using the sanitizing solution recommended by the manufacturer.
- When the sanitizing cycle is complete (in approximately 15 minutes), turn the switch from the WASH or CLEAN position to the ICE or ON position.

ICE STORAGE BIN   While the ice machine is cleaning and sanitizing, clean the ice storage bin which has already been emptied. Use a solution of a half cup of baking soda per 1 gallon of warm water. Rinse the bin and sanitize it with a solution of one teaspoon of household bleach per quart of warm water. Do not use strong detergents, appliance polishes, or finish preservatives in cleaning the interior portion of the bin.

Maintenance

In addition to cleaning and sanitizing the ice machine and ice storage bin, it is also necessary to clean the condenser (assuming it is an air-cooled machine), on a monthly basis (see Figure 7.12). A dirty condenser reduces the capacity of ice production in the machine and also shortens the life of the condenser. *Note:* Prior to cleaning the condenser, disconnect the flow of electric power to the machine.

Clean the condenser fins either with a soft brush or with a vacuum and brush attachment. Be careful not to bend the condenser fins. Should they become bent, they should be straightened with a fin comb. If the brush or vacuum does not adequately clean the fins, either blow compressed air from the inside through the fins or clean the fins with a commercial condenser coil cleaner.

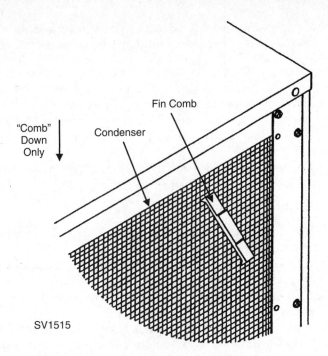

SV1515

FIGURE 7.12 Cleaning the condenser of an ice machine using a fin comb.

Source: Kolpak.

The fan blades should also be cleaned at this time. Use a damp cloth to wipe the blades and the exterior of the motor. Do not allow water to get into the motor.

Check waterlines and fittings for leaks. Make sure that the tubing is not rubbing or vibrating against other tubing or panels.

CARBONATED BEVERAGE DISPENSER

Overview

There are two types of carbonated beverage dispensers: premix and postmix. While quite different in how they dispense beverages, the cleaning and maintenance are essentially the same; hence they are covered together. Major repairs on either design should be performed only by qualified factory-trained mechanics.

PREMIX   In a premix system, the carbonated beverage is delivered to the food-service operation completely mixed in 5-gallon containers. The product in boxes, ready to use, is identical to the soda you would purchase in a grocery store in a 1-liter bottle. The only difference is the method of dispensing the product. While it is fairly easy to pick up a chilled 1-liter bottle and pour it into a glass of ice, 5 gallons is a different matter. That fact, along with the need to maintain product integrity and pour it at the proper temperature, means that some additional equipment is needed.

To commercially dispense carbonated beverages: A CO_2 tank is hooked up to a series of boxes of carbonated beverages. When a button or lever is pushed on the dispensing head, the CO_2 pushes the product from the box, through a chilling device, and on to the dispensing valve, where it goes into a glass or cup of ice.

The chiller that it passes through can be either an electrical mechanical chiller or a cooling plate located in the bottom of the ice bin. If a cooling plate is used, no electricity is needed. Since the product is already mixed, no water is needed. Therefore, with the use of a cooling plate, the entire operation can be portable. Hence, premix setups are very popular with portable bars used at banquets and for soft drink stands at fairs and sporting events.

POSTMIX The dispensing of postmix carbonated beverages is a little more complicated. It also uses 5-gallon boxes, but they contain pure syrup only:

- The syrup lines go through a chiller and then on to the dispensing valve.
- Incoming tap water goes through a filter process, then on to the chiller, and on to the carbonator where it picks up its effervescence.
- The carbonated water then goes on to the dispensing valve, where it is mixed with the chilled syrup, usually at a ratio of 5 parts of carbonated water to 1 part of syrup.
- The mixed beverage then goes into the customer's glass or cup of ice.

SIMILARITIES AND DIFFERENCES

- Both use 5-gallon boxes. Premix is completely mixed and ready to serve. Postmix contains only syrup in the box.
- Both are cooled so that the product going into the glass or cup is below 40°F (4°C).
- Both use CO_2 tanks and have connector valves, chillers, and dispensing valves. Postmix, in addition, has a carbonator.
- Both use the same type of dispensing heads, of which there are two types.
  - One is a hand-held device with buttons commonly known as a "bar gun." Each button corresponds to a particular flavor of beverage. When the button is pushed, the product is dispensed.
  - The second is a tower style box with a lever for each dispensing head, which represents each flavor of beverage. When the lever is pushed, product is dispensed (see Figure 7.13).
- With postmix, the syrup and carbonated water is mixed in the dispensing head and distributed. In premix, the product is merely distributed.
- Premix can be completely portable if it is using a chiller plate submerged in ice. Postmix—because it needs an incoming water line, drain, and electricity—is a permanent installation.
- While postmix has a higher initial investment cost because of additional equipment, the product is much less expensive to purchase than premix. As a result, postmix gives a higher gross profit than premix and is thus the more popular of the two systems.
- The external characteristics of the two systems are so similar that your employees probably wouldn't know the difference and probably wouldn't care.

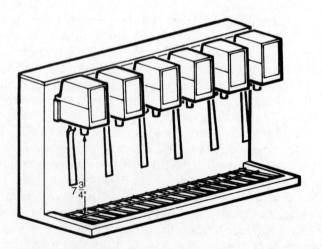

FIGURE 7.13 Carbonated beverage dispenser.
Source: Multiplex Co.

Parts

PREMIX

Connector valve—A device that connects the beverage box to the syrup line.

Syrup line—Plastic tubing through which the carbonated beverage flows from the box to the dispensing head.

Chilling plate—A metal plate, submerged in ice, through which the carbonated beverage line passes to cool the beverage to less than 40°F (4°C).

Chiller—An electrical device that the carbonated beverage passes through, chilling the product to less than 40°F (4°C). Premix systems operate with either a chilling plate or an electrical chiller.

Dispensing head—A valve that allows the carbonated beverage to flow from the box to the glass or cup.

POSTMIX

Connector valve—The device that connects the syrup box to the syrup line.

Syrup line—Plastic tubing through which the syrup flows from the box to the dispensing head.

Carbonator—A device that takes filtered water and carbonates it to give the water effervescence.

Chiller—An electrical device that the syrup and carbonated water pass through (in separate lines) chilling them to less than 40°F (4°C).

Dispensing head—A valve that takes syrup and carbonated water, mixes them in a ratio of 1 part syrup to 5 parts water, and then dispenses the final product.

Operation

As far as the operation of the equipment is concerned, both premix and postmix systems operate identically.

Two lines are hooked up to each box with connecting valves. The first line valve (the one that carries the syrup or beverage) is pushed down over the box valve and twisted until it is seated on the box valve. The second line (the one carrying the CO_2) is connected in the same manner. The beverage/syrup line valve has three inserts, while the CO_2 line has two inserts, thus making it impossible to hook the wrong line to the wrong valve on a particular box.

A problem arises in that the beverage/syrup line can be hooked up to the wrong box, resulting in the wrong flavor being dispensed from the dispensing head. To overcome this, each beverage/syrup line should be tagged, naming the flavor of the box to which it should be attached.

Once the lines are hooked up properly, the only thing left for the operator to do is to dispense the product. This is done by the operator putting ice into the glass or cup. The product is then dispensed into the glass or cup by pushing the proper button on a handheld device or by pushing the proper lever on a tower device.

Cleaning

DAILY

- Remove the nozzles and diffusers from the dispensing valves. Clean them with warm (not hot) water and soap. Rinse with carbonated water and reinstall. It is extremely important to do this because the sugar from the syrup develops into a slimy bacterial growth that is not only unsightly, but potentially dangerous.

- Clean all dispenser drain housings with soap and warm water. Wash the drain rack in the pot and pan sink. Pour hot water down the drain.
- Clean the syrup box storage area. Check the syrup connector valves for leaks and clean around the connectors with soap and warm water. Rinse off all soap. When hooking up a fresh box/tank of syrup, clean the inside of the syrup connector with soap and warm water. Thoroughly rinse off all soap.

Maintenance

DAILY   Take the temperature of the finished drinks by pouring out the first drink and taking the temperature of the second drink. The temperature should be 40°F (4°C) or less.

QUARTERLY   Inspect syrup lines for proper flavor identification labels. Replace labels if necessary.

Using a Brix cup and syrup separator, check for proper carbonated water flow, which should be 5 ounces in four seconds. Also check for proper syrup-to-water ratios, normally 1:5. If either of these rates is not at their proper level, call a qualified person to adjust the system. In addition to a Brix cup and syrup separator, a refractometer can be used to measure the syrup to water ratio.

If the refrigeration unit is equipped with an air-cooled condenser, clean it with a vacuum cleaner.

Note: The entire carbonated beverage system should be thoroughly inspected by a competent carbonated beverage specialist every three months. Leading syrup manufacturers (e.g., Coca Cola, Pepsi Cola, and others) normally provide this service at no charge to their customers.

Questions

1. Explain in your own words how a refrigeration system works.
2. How is a refrigeration thermometer calibrated?
3. What maintenance is required on a reach-in refrigerator?
4. On a typical walk-in door panel, other than the door, what other components are located on the panel?
5. Explain how an ice machine makes ice.
6. Discuss the differences between a premix and postmix carbonated beverage dispenser.

Project

Obtain the owner's manual for the ice machine located in your lab. Study it carefully and demonstrate how to clean and sanitize the interior of the machine.

Acknowledgments

The Delfield Company, Mount Pleasant, MI.
Kold-Draft, Erie, PA.
Kolpak Walk-Ins, Franklin, TN.

Lern Inc., Chicago, IL.
Multiplex Company Inc., Ballwin, MO.

Web Sites

Beverage-Air
www.beverage-air.com

The Delfield Company
www.delfield.com

Hoshizaki American Inc.
www.hoshizaki.com

Hussmann Corporation
www.hussmann.com

Manitowoc Ice Inc.
www.manitowocice.com

McCall Refrigeration
www.mccallrefrigeration.com

Kold-Draft
www.kold-draft.com

Kolpak Walk-Ins
www.kolpak.com

Multiplex Company Inc.
www.multiplex-beverage.com

Scotsman Ice Systems
www.scotsman-ice.com

Traulsen & Co. Inc.
www.traulsen.com

True Food Service Equipment Inc.
www.truemfg.com

Resources

Birchfield, John C. (1998). Design and Layout of Foodservice Facilities. New York, NY: John Wiley & Sons, Inc.

Katsigris, Costas & Thomas, Chris (1999). Design and Equipment for Restaurants and Foodservice: A Management View. New York, NY: John Wiley & Sons, Inc.

Kazarian, Edward A. (1997). Foodservice Facilities Planning, 3rd ed. New York, NY: John Wiley & Sons, Inc.

Scriven, C. & Stevens, J. (1982). Food Equipment Facts. New York, NY: John Wiley & Sons, Inc.

Product specification sheets and owners manual from the following companies:

Arctic Temp Inc.

Bally Refrigerated Boxes

The Delfield Co.

Kold-Draft

Kolpac Walk ins Inc.

Lern Inc.

Manitowoc Ice Inc.

McCall Refrigeration Inc.

Multiplex Beverage Co.

Traulson & Co., Inc.

CHAPTER 8

Sanitation Equipment

Objectives

Upon completion of this chapter, you will be able to:

- Discuss the various types of dishwashers and the applications of each.
- Demonstrate how to assemble, disassemble, and operate a dishwasher.
- Describe the proper procedure for operating a pot and pan sink.
- Discuss the advantages of having a garbage disposal. Explain how to operate one and the limitations of the mechanism.

Key Terms

booster heater
clean dish table
clean drain board
high-temperature dishwasher
low-temperature dishwasher

prerinse
reset button
soiled dish table
soiled drain board

INTRODUCTION

In this chapter, we will look at the machinery that cleans and sanitizes the equipment, utensils, china, glassware, and flatware. This consists of the dishwasher, the pot and pan sink, and disposers.

Dishwashers come in several styles: under-counter, one-tank, two-tank, and three-tank. Another style is the carrousel that is essentially a three-tank machine with a curved soiled and clean dish table, resembling a carrousel (see Figure 8.1). The under-counter dishwasher is essentially the same as the dishwasher in your home. It has a limited use commercially, as its capacity is restricted and is used only in very low-volume operations. The two-tank machine is a hybrid of the one-tank and the three-tank. Its operation is virtually the same as a one-tank machine. Therefore, in this chapter we will focus on the one-tank and three-tank dishwashers.

All dishwashers have several things in common. First and foremost, the primary purpose of a dishwasher is to clean and sanitize soiled dishes for reuse in the operation. The key words are "clean" and "sanitize." Dishes are cleaned primarily by water pressure. While detergents are used to loosen the soil on the dishes, the water pressure ultimately cleans them. Most commercial dishwashers have water coming out of the wash arms at 15–20 pounds per square inch (PSI) and this pressure removes the soil.

The dishes are then sanitized by either high water temperature or chemicals. Thus there are two types of dishwashers: high-temperature and low-temperature. While their operating characteristics are essentially the same, the means of sanitizing are vastly different. **High-temperature dishwashers** sanitize by killing bacteria with heat. They do this in the final rinse cycle when the dishes are rinsed with clear water that is at 180°F (83°C). **Low-temperature dishwashers**, on the other hand, sanitize by using chemicals and have a maximum temperature of 135°F (58°C). Notice that the temperature on the high-temp machine is a minimum and the temperature on the low-temp machine is a maximum. On

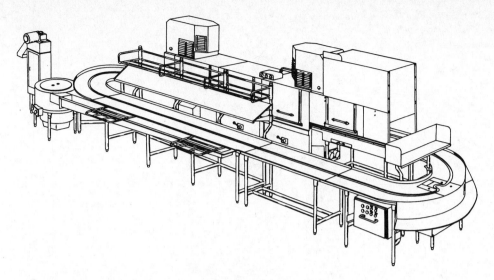

FIGURE 8.1 A carrousel dish setup. Soiled dishes are loaded and clean dishes are unloaded in the same area.

Source: Hobart.

the low-temp machine, this is to avoid having the chemicals being dissipated by evaporation.

With the exception of the under-counter model, all dishwashing operations have two other components: a soiled dish table and a clean dish table.

The **soiled dish table** is where the dishes, glassware, and flatware from the dining room are sorted. Left-over food is scraped from the dishes and, in the case of a one-tank or two-tank machine, is prerinsed. Glassware is sorted and placed in glass racks and flatware is presoaked. (These procedures are covered in more detail later.) The soiled dish area also has a garbage disposal as part of its makeup.

The **clean dish table** is where the dishes come out of the dishwasher and are left to air dry. They are then placed into lowerators, or dish "dollies," and taken to their place of use. Since the dishes coming out of a low-temp machine do not dry as quickly as the dishes out of a high-temp machine, the clean dish table for a low-temp machine is normally longer to accommodate the delay in air drying.

While some dishwashers do a better job than others, the key to a successful dishwashing operation is the proper use and maintenance of the equipment.

ONE-TANK DISHWASHER

Overview

One-tank (or single-tank) dishwashers are normally used in smaller operations that serve up to 250 meals per hour. Larger operations use a two-tank or three-tank machine. In a one-tank operation, the dishes are sorted on the soiled dish table, scraped clean, racked, and rinsed with a prerinse hose. The racks are manually placed into and removed from the machine as opposed to a conveyer used in the two- and three-tank machines (see Figure 8.2).

Parts

- Drain lever—Opens and closes the drain to the tank. When the drain lever is in the up position, the drain is open. Conversely, when it is down, the drain is closed.
- Control box—The panel that contains the POWER switch and the WASH/RINSE switch (see Figure 8.3). On newer models, a digital readout tells which operational mode the machine is currently in and gives the temperature of the water during each cycle.

FIGURE 8.2
Source: Hobart.

- POWER switch—Turns the dishwasher on and takes it through the wash, rinse, and final rinse cycles. On most machines, the power switch stays in the ON position during the entire shift. When the doors are opened, the machine automatically shuts off; when the doors are closed, the machine starts up. *Note*: On manually operated machines, the WASH switch is manually depressed for the wash cycle and the RINSE switch is manually depressed for the rinse cycle.
- Pump motor—Causes the water to be forced up into the wash and rinse arms at high pressure.
- **Booster heater**—Takes water from the hot water line and heats it to 180°F (83°C).
- Inspection door—The door located on the front of the machine that facilitates access for cleaning and correcting occasional jams inside the machine.

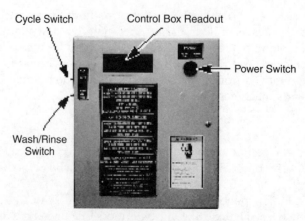

FIGURE 8.3 Control box for a one-tank dishwasher.
Source: Hobart.

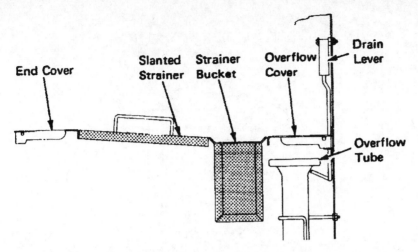

FIGURE 8.4 The proper setup of parts for a one-tank dishwasher.
Source: Hobart.

Note: On most models the side doors used for sliding trays in and out of the machine do not close if the inspection door is in the up position.

- Wash arm—The part that the water flows through at high pressure to clean the dishes. The wash arm rotates to spray water throughout the washing tank chamber.
- Rinse arm—The part that the hot rinse water goes through at high pressure. It also rotates to allow the rinse water to circulate throughout the wash tank chamber.

Operation

The previous shift should have the dishwasher properly set up and ready to go. However, check and make sure that the following are in place (see Figure 8.4):

> The overflow tube
>
> The overflow cover
>
> The end cover
>
> The slanted strainer
>
> The strainer bucket

To operate the dishwasher, do the following:

- If the machine is equipped with an automatic detergent and/or rinse dispenser, make sure that the dispensers are filled with detergent and rinse additives (see Figures 8.5 and 8.6). If the machine does not have an automatic dispenser, scatter the initial charge of detergent on the slanted strainer.
- Check the drain lever and make sure that the drain is closed. (On some models, when the doors to the machine are closed, the drain automatically closes.)
- Close all doors.
- Push the power switch to ON. On most models, the machine automatically fills with water. On older models, push the FILL switch to fill the machine with water. If the machine does not fill with water, check the cycle switch. It should be in the AUTOMATIC position, with the WASH/RINSE switch in the OFF position. Once the machine is filled with water, it is ready to receive dishes.
- Manually scrape the left-over food off the dishes into the garbage can. Use a rubber scraper. Do not use steel wool or metal sponges to perform this task. These can cause microscopic grooves in the dishes that can harbor bacteria.
- Rack the dishes by placing the plates and dishes upright in a peg rack. Do not stack dishes on top of one another or allow them to touch. The spray must be

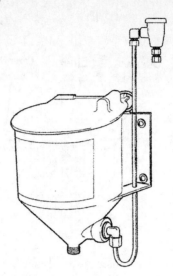

FIGURE 8.5 Automatic detergent dispenser for a dishwasher.

Source: Ecolab.

able to hit all surfaces of the dishes. Because the cleaning is done by water pressure, the water must have access to all sides of every dish (see Figure 8.7).

• **Prerinse** the dishes with the prerinse hose after racking and before placing them into the machine.

• Cups, glasses, and bowls should be inverted in an open flat rack or compartment rack.

• Silverware should be presoaked, scattered on a flat rack, washed, rinsed, sorted by implement type, placed into plastic cylinders business side down, rewashed, and rerinsed.

• After filling a rack, open the door and slide the rack into the dish machine. *Note:* When the loading door is opened, the unloading door opens simultaneously. When the rack is in the machine, close the door. On most models, when the door is closed, the unit automatically goes through the wash cycle, rinse

FIGURE 8.6 Automatic sanitizing dispenser for a dishwasher.

Source: Ecolab.

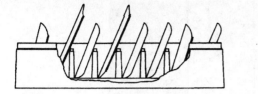 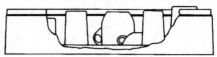

FIGURE 8.7   Proper racking procedure for plates (left) and cups and glasses (right).
Source: Hobart.

cycle, and the final rinse cycle. On other models, the wash and final rinse cycles each have a switch that must be manually pushed to activate the cycle. In this case, the wash cycle should last for a minimum of 40 seconds and the rinse cycle for a minimum of 18 seconds.

- When the wash and rinse cycles are completed, open the doors, remove the rack with the clean dishes, slide a rack of soiled dishes into the machine, and close the doors. If for any reason you need to open the door while the machine is in one of its cycles, turn the power switch to the OFF position. Then wait ten seconds before opening the doors to allow the wash or rinse arm to coast down to avoid splashing hot water.

Cleaning

After each shift, the dishwasher should be thoroughly cleaned:

- Turn the power switch to the OFF position. If the machine has steam heat, turn off the steam valve.
- Open the doors to the machine.
- Squeegee the water and soil from the dish tables into the dishwasher. Clean the dish tables with a cloth and a nonabrasive cleaner diluted according to the manufacturer's directions.
- If the soiled dish table is equipped with a scrap sink, remove the glide rails and clean these in the pot and pan sink. Empty the crumb strainer and wipe the sink down with the same solution used for the dish table.
- Drain the machine by pulling the drain lever.
- Remove and empty the slanted strainer and the strainer bucket. Wash and rinse them in the pot and pan sink.
- Raise the overflow cover and remove the overflow tube. Wash and rinse the inside and outside of the overflow tube in the pot and pan sink.
- Spray the interior of the machine with the prerinse hose. Thoroughly clean the inside of the machine with a cloth or soft sponge and diluted nonabrasive cleanser. Never use steel wool or a metal sponge to clean any part of the dishwasher or the dish tables. Be sure to clean the undersides of the tray glide. Rinse again.
- Never allow food to collect on the bottom of the tank.
- Replace all parts that have been removed.
- Leave the machine doors open to allow the interior of the machine to air dry.

  The dishwasher is now ready for the next shift.

Maintenance

The wash pump motor contains permanently lubricated bearings; no additional lubrication is necessary.

Daily, check the upper and lower wash and rinse arms to see that the nozzles are free from any lime deposits, solids, or obstructions. If the slanted strainer or the strainer bucket is not seated properly, food particles or bones can get into the wash arm and clog the nozzles.

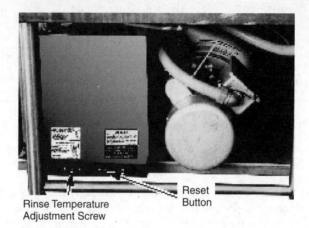

Rinse Temperature
Adjustment Screw

Reset
Button

FIGURE 8.8   RESET button on a dishwasher motor.
Source: Hobart.

To clean the wash or rinse arms:

- Turn off the power supply to both the dishwasher and the booster heater.
- Remove the lower rinse arm by lifting it off and then unscrew the bearing pin on the lower wash arm and lift it off.
- Unscrew the hand knob on the upper rinse and wash arm and remove them.
- Inspect the wash arms and remove any obstructions. Check for any lime deposit buildup. If a buildup exists, soak the arms in a de-liming solution, following the manufacturer's instructions.
- After the arms have been properly cleaned and de-limed, they should be replaced. To check if they have been replaced properly, twirl the wash and rinse arms. They should rotate freely and continue to turn for a few seconds.

Occasionally, the pump motor can become overheated. When this occurs, a thermal overload causes the pump to cease operation. Most dishwashers are equipped with a manual reset button normally located on the bottom of the pump motor (see Figure 8.8). To restart the motor, allow it to cool first and then depress the RESET button.

On dishwashers equipped with a gas tank heater and/or a gas booster heater, check the flue every three months to make sure that there are no obstructions or leaks.

THREE-TANK DISHWASHER

Overview

The operating characteristics of the three-tank dish machine are the same as for a one-tank machine, that is, a wash cycle, rinse cycle, and final rinse cycle. In addition, three-tank machines have a prerinse cycle. Also, the three-tank machine has more working parts, simply because it is larger and handles more volume. In addition to the four cycles, some three-tank machines have a blower/dryer at the end of the procedure to speed the drying process of the dishes.

All three-tank dishwashers are automatically fed, that is, the racks are carried into and through the machine. Unlike the one-tank machine, where the rack is manually pushed into and manually retrieved from the machine, the three-tank machine runs on a conveyor system (see Figure 8.9).

On some models, the racks are placed in the dishwasher where hooks on a ratchet-type device grab the rack and pull it through the machine (similar to a car wash, where a hook is put on your car and it is then pulled through the wash).

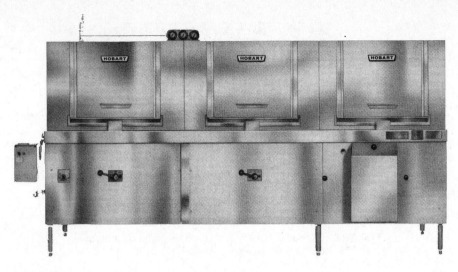

FIGURE 8.9

Source: Hobart.

Most machines, however, run on a conveyor belt that has plastic "teeth." These dishwashers are often called flight machines. The dishes are placed between the teeth in an inclining position. Glasses, cups, and silverware still need to be placed in racks and the racks are then set on the teeth.

Parts

- Pump intake screen—Keeps debris away from the pump, so that the water pumped into the spray arms does not clog nozzles, thus preventing the dishwasher from working properly.
- Strainer pans—Prevents debris from falling into the tank. It is slanted so that the debris falls into the strainer basket.
- Strainer basket—Collects the debris from the strainer pan. Should be emptied periodically throughout the washing process.
- Flush arm—Located at the loading end of the dishwasher, this arm prerinses or flushes the dishes prior to the washing process. Water from the tank is pumped into the flush arm and is sprayed at a high rate of pounds per square inch (PSI).
- Wash arms—Located in the wash tank and works in the same manner as the flush arm; it only washes the dishes with water pressure aided by detergent.
- Rinse arms—Located in the rinse tank to rinse the dishes, often injected with a rinse additive to avoid spotting on dishes.
- Curtains—Located at both ends of the dishwasher to prevent water from spraying out into the kitchen. Also located between the tanks to prevent detergent from getting into the rinse tank and the rinse additive from getting into the wash tank.
- Power switch—Turns the electrical power to the dishwasher on or off. If the machine is equipped with a blower/dryer, it may be activated by this switch or it could have its own ON/OFF switch.
- START/STOP switch(es)—Starts and stops the conveyer belt. Some machines are equipped with an automatic stop after several minutes pass with nothing being loaded into the machine.
- Trip assembly—Stops the conveyer belt when dishes reach the end of the belt at the unloading end of the dishwasher. When the last dish is removed, the belt restarts (see Figure 8.10).
- Thermometers—Located on the control panel, the thermometers give the temperature of each of the four dishwashing functions (see Figure 8.11).

FIGURE 8.10 Proper racking procedure for plates on a flight machine. If the person unloading gets behind, the last plate (left) will stop the belt.

Source: Hobart.

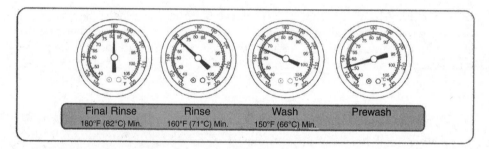

| Final Rinse | Rinse | Wash | Prewash |
| 180°F (82°C) Min. | 160°F (71°C) Min. | 150°F (66°C) Min. | |

FIGURE 8.11 Thermometers on a three-tank machine.

Source: Hobart.

Operation

The dishwasher should be set up properly by the previous shift. However, before filling it, check the following parts to make sure that they are properly installed:

- Pump intake screens should be installed at each pump intake (see Figure 8.12).
- Strainer pans should be in place and cover each tank.
- Strainer baskets should be in place in strainer pans.
- Check end caps at the end of the wash arms to ascertain that they are tightly screwed on (see Figure 8.13).
- Check wash arms to see if they are properly installed and latched in place.

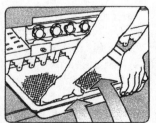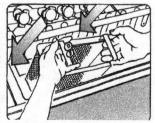

FIGURE 8.12 The screens and strainer pans and baskets should be in place prior to starting the machine.

Source: Hobart.

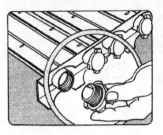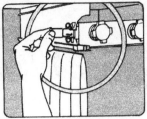

FIGURE 8.13 Check to see if the end caps and wash arms are properly installed.

Source: Hobart.

- Check the flush arm at the loading end of the machine for proper installation.
- Make sure that the final rinse arm is properly installed (see Figure 8.14).
- Check to see that the final rinse actuators move freely.
- Make sure that all curtains are in their proper places (see Figure 8.15).

After all the parts are correctly assembled, the washing procedure is as follows:

- Close all doors and drains.
- Turn on the power switch for the dishwasher. If the machine is equipped with a blower/dryer, turn on that also. (On most models, the blower/dryer is a separate switch.)
- Press the FILL button, if necessary. (On most models the machine automatically fills when the power switch is activated.)
- When the machine is filled, on most models a light indicates that it is ready for use. Filling takes several minutes. The dishwasher maintains the proper water levels throughout the washing process as well as the proper temperature for each function.
- Press the START button to activate the conveyer and the pumps. Depending on the model, the START button could be located either on the control panel, or on the loading end of the machine, or on the unloading end, or sometimes at all three locations. The STOP button, which stops the conveyer and the pumps, is located by the START button.
- Prescrape dishes to remove any left-over food, paper napkins, etc. Do not use steel wool. It is not necessary to prerinse dishes since the machine does this function.
- If using a flight machine, place all plates, saucers, and trays in an inclined position between the teeth on the conveyer. Place bowls upside down on the teeth. Cups, glasses, and silverware should be placed in racks and then placed on the teeth on the conveyer.
- Remove dishes from the conveyer at the unloading end of the machine and place them in or on dish storage racks or lowerators. Should the person

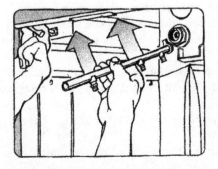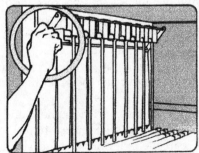

FIGURE 8.14 Check the final rinse arms.

Source: Hobart.

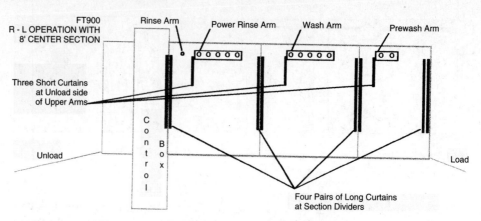

FIGURE 8.15 Long and short curtain placement on a three-tank machine.

Source: Hobart.

unloading get behind, a trip assembly at the end of the conveyer automatically stops the conveyer and shuts down the pumps. When the dish is removed from the trip assembly, the conveyer and pumps restart.

- During the washing process, it is necessary to empty the strainer baskets from time to time. Should they become clogged; the dishwasher will not work properly. Stop the machine and open the side doors. Remove the strainer baskets, empty them, and return them to their respective positions. Close the doors and start the dishwasher again.
- Throughout the dishwashing process, check the thermometers of the various functions to ascertain that the proper water temperatures are being maintained.

Cleaning

After each shift, the dishwasher must be thoroughly cleaned.

- Turn the power switch to OFF.
- Open the drain levers for each tank (located on the front of the machine near the floor). Draining takes several minutes.
- Remove and clean the curtains.
- Hose down the loading and unloading shelf. Spray the debris into the dishwasher.
- Remove the wash arms and the end caps on the wash arms. Clean the wash arms in the pot and pan sink. Return the end caps to the wash arms and do not overtighten them.
- Remove the flush arm at the loading end of the machine and clean it in the pot and pan sink. Make sure that the nozzles in the flush arm are clean.
- Remove the strainer baskets and the strainer pans; empty them in the trash can. Do not bang them to dislodge debris; this bends them and they will not fit back into the dishwasher. Scrub the strainer baskets and strainer pans in the pot and pan sink.
- Remove the pump intake screens and clean them in the pot and pan sink.
- Remove and clean the final rinse arms. Clean the nozzles with a straightened paper clip.
- Rinse the tanks with the hose and remove any debris that may have fallen into the tank (see Figure 8.16).
- Clean the exterior of the dishwasher with a nonabrasive stainless steel cleaner. Do not use steel wool to clean any part of the dishwasher.
- Reinstall the wash arms, flush arm, strainer pan, strainer basket, pump intake screens, final rinse arms, and curtains. Leave the access doors open.

  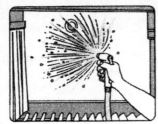

FIGURE 8.16 Proper cleaning procedure for a three-tank machine.

Source: Hobart.

Maintenance

All the motors have sealed bearings and therefore require no lubrication. The oil level in the gear motor that runs the conveyor should be checked every six months.

The top cover and the duct on the top of the dishwasher should be cleaned every two weeks. If the machine is equipped with a blower/dryer, the filter should be cleaned bimonthly.

In areas with hard water, the machine should be de-scaled and de-limed weekly.

POT AND PAN SINK

Overview

One of the most detested and yet one of the most important jobs in the kitchen is cleaning pots and pans. While it is considered a "no-brainer" job, remember that the person washing the pot and pans must use the correct chemicals, maintain the correct water temperature, keep track of the amount of time that a utensil is in the sanitizing solution, and physically clean the utensil properly. The job is more complicated than most people realize. Also keep in mind that, if any of this is not done correctly, contamination could occur (see Figure 8.17).

Parts

- **Soiled drain board**—The area where soiled pots and pans are placed prior to cleaning.
- Wash sink—Compartment where soiled pots and pans are washed.
- Rinse sink—Compartment where the detergent is rinsed off the clean pots and pans.

FIGURE 8.17

- Sanitizing sink—Compartment where the pot and pans are sanitized.
- **Clean drain board**—The area where the clean and sanitized pots and pans are air-dried.
- Faucets—The device that dispatches the hot and cold potable water into the sink. Faucets can be either stationary, where a faucet is required over each sink, or a swing faucet that can be directed to two or more sinks.
- Crumb strainer—The device that prevents garbage from going down the drains when the sink is emptied.

Operation

- Dirty pots and pans should be prerinsed, with all excess soil and food removed to keep the wash water as clean as possible.
- They are then placed on the soiled drain.
- The wash water should contain a detergent mixed according to the manufacturer's directions and be a minimum of 110°F (44°C). Most pot and pan sinks have automatic dispensers that dispense the correct amount of detergent (see Figure 8.18).
- The utensil should be scrubbed, removing all soil from both its inside and outside. When the suds disappear, empty the sink, clean it out, and start over with hot clean water and the proper amount of detergent.
- After washing, the utensil is then rinsed in clear water at 110°F (44°C). It is important that all the detergent be removed in the rinsing procedure so as not to inhibit the sanitizer from working properly.
- After rinsing, the utensil goes into the sanitizing sink with a solution of chlorine, iodine, or quaternary ammonium, mixed according to the manufacturer's directions. The utensils should be sanitized for a minimum of 60 seconds. Most pot and pan sinks have automatic dispensers that dispense the correct amount of sanitizer (see Figure 8.19).

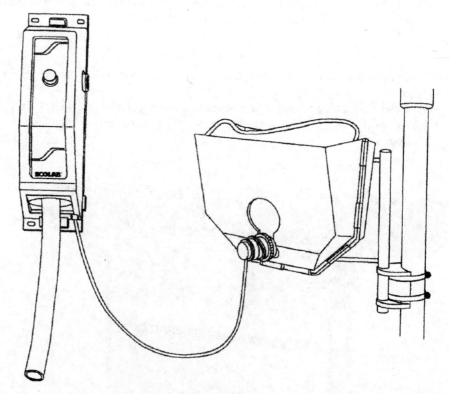

FIGURE 8.18 Automatic detergent dispenser for a pot and pan sink.

Source: Ecolab.

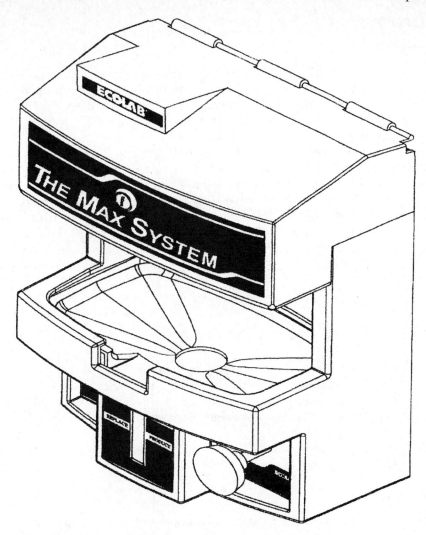

FIGURE 8.19 Automatic sanitizing dispenser for a pot and pan sink.

Source: Ecolab.

- A test kit should be used periodically to ascertain that the sanitizer is of sufficient strength to do its job.
- If a sanitizer is not used, the utensil must be immersed in hot water [180°F (83°C)] for 30 seconds.
- The utensil then goes to the clean drain board to be air-dried. Do not hand-dry with a towel as this could contaminate the utensil.

Cleaning

After each use, the pot and pan sink should be thoroughly cleaned. Drain all three compartments. Empty the soil out of the crumb strainers. Clean the sinks using a nonabrasive pad. Do not use steel wool. Make sure that the wash sink and the sanitizer sink are completely rinsed since the chemicals used in the detergent and sanitizer will eventually corrode the stainless steel.

Maintenance

There is no maintenance to be performed on the pot and pan sink.

If automatic dispensers are used for the detergent and sanitizer, they should be periodically checked by the company supplying them to verify that the correct amount of detergent and sanitizer is being dispensed.

DISPOSERS

Overview

The disposer takes "soft" garbage and cuts, grinds, and reduces it to a pulp. It is an environment-friendly piece of kitchen equipment that reduces debris so that it can be sent down the drain into the sewage system where it is treated. By using disposers in the kitchen, vast amounts of garbage stay out of the landfill (see Figure 8.20).

The type of debris it can take is limited. A rule of thumb is that the larger the disposer, the higher the horsepower, the greater range of goods it can grind. Small disposers with a low horsepower will only grind soft foods such as produce, while very large ones with a high horsepower can grind harder foods such as bones. Disposers operate with metal teeth on a rotor that turns at a high rate of rotations minute (RPM) that cut and pulverize the garbage. This is flushed down the drain and into the sewage system. Disposers are normally located in the dishwashing scrapping area, pot and pan sinks, and vegetable prep sinks.

Parts

- Control panel—Houses the START button (switch) and the STOP button (switch).
- Cone—The basin between the sink top and the disposer to collect garbage prior to being pushed into the disposal (see Figure 8.21).
- **Reset button**—Allows the motor to be restarted if it has been shut down due to overheating. This happens when too much debris or a foreign object is put into the disposer.
- Rotor—The cutting device inside the disposer that cuts and grinds the garbage.

Operation

Water is an integral part of the disposal process. With some disposers, the water source is turned on automatically when the disposer is started. On other models, the water must be manually turned on prior to the disposer being turned on.

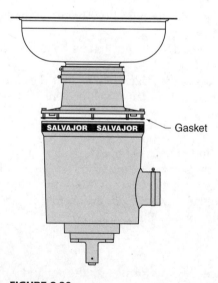

FIGURE 8.20

Source: Salvajor.

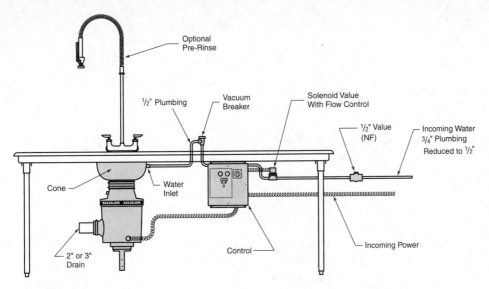

FIGURE 8.21 Soiled dish table for a one-tank dishwasher showing the prerinse operation and parts of a disposer.

Source: Salvajor.

Do not attempt to operate a disposer without water running directly into it in a steady stream. To properly operate a disposer:

- Push the START button on the control panel.
- Make sure that there is a steady stream of water going into the disposer.
- Feed garbage into the disposer in a steady continuous flow. Do not overload the unit with an excess amount of debris. **Keep your hands away from the disposer**.
- When all the garbage has been run through the disposer, allow the unit to run for three minutes, with the water running, to clear itself of all ground debris.
- Push the STOP button on the control panel to stop the disposer.

Do not put the following into a disposer as they could be expelled from the unit and cause injury:

- Clam or oyster shells.
- Glass, china, or plastic.
- Metal such as bottle caps, aluminum foil, tin cans, knives, forks, or spoons.
- Drain cleaner or other caustic cleaners.

Occasionally, the disposer will stop while it is in operation, either because it is overloaded or an object has caused it to jam. When this happens:

- Depress the STOP button.
- Turn off the electrical supply by flipping the circuit breaker to the OFF position at the electrical panel.
- Free the rotor from its jammed condition by reversing the rotor rotation. This should be done using a de-jamming tool supplied with the disposer or a long wooden stick. When released, the rotor should move freely.
- Remove all foreign material that caused the jam.
- Wait several minutes to allow the motor to cool down.
- Depress the RESET button that is located on the bottom of the disposer. Turn the electrical supply ON at the electrical panel.
- Depress the START button (see Figure 8.22).

FIGURE 8.22 RESET button for a disposer.

Source: Salvajor.

Cleaning

The exterior of the disposer can be cleaned with a damp towel. If heavily stained, a nonabrasive cleaner or mild detergent can be used.

The interior of the unit self-cleans when the disposer is left running for three minutes after all the debris has been sent through.

Maintenance

There is no maintenance to be performed on the disposer.

Questions

1. Explain how a high-temperature dishwasher and a low-temperature dishwasher sanitize dishes.
2. Discuss the different styles of dishwashers.
3. What is a booster heater? Why is it important?
4. Explain the purpose of having three basins in a pot and pan sink.
5. How often should the water be changed in a pot and pan sink?
6. Explain how a garbage disposal works.

Project

Play the role of a foodservice manager and train a new employee in the procedure of checking that the dishwasher in your lab is set up properly. Train them on the correct procedure to rack, prerinse, wash, and dry dishes. Show them how to disassemble and clean the dishwasher.

Acknowledgments

Ecolab Inc., St. Paul, MN.
Hobart Corporation, Troy, OH.
Metal Master Food Service Equipment Inc., Smyrna, DE.
Salvajor Corporation, Kansas City, MO.

Web Sites

Blakeslee
www.blakesleeinc.com

Ecolab Inc.
www.ecolab.com

Hobart Corporation
www.hobartcorp.com

Jackson MSC
www.jacksonmsc.com

The Stero Company
www.stero.com

Salvajor Corporation
www.salvajor.com

Resources

Birchfield, John C. (1998). Design and Layout of Foodservice Facilities. New York, NY: John Wiley & Sons, Inc.

Katsigris, Costas & Thomas, Chris (1999). Design and Equipment for Restaurants and Food-service: A Management View. New York, NY: John Wiley & Sons, Inc.

Kazarian, Edward A. (1997). Foodservice Facilities Planning, 3rd ed. New York, NY: John Wiley & Sons, Inc.

Scriven, C. & Stevens, J. (1982). Food Equipment Facts. New York, NY: John Wiley & Sons, Inc.

Product specification sheets and owners manual from the following companies:

Ecolab Inc.

Hobart Corporation

Jackson MSC

Metal Masters Foodservice Equipment Co.

The Salvajor Company

APPENDIX

The Competency verification sheet should be signed by the classroom/lab instructor or by the food service manager. The student or the employee should also sign it. By virtue of both signatures, the instructor/manager and the student/employee acknowledge that the student has been trained and understands the safe operation of the piece of equipment signed for. Additional pieces of equipment may be added to the list.

Competency Verification Sheet		
Equipment	**Instructor**	**Student**
Mixer		
Slicer		
Cutter mixer		
Deep fat fryer		
Pressure steamer		
Braising pan		
Dishwasher		
Disposal		

INDEX